Tears Of Sadness, Tears Of Gladness

Gospel Sermons For Lent/Easter

Cycle A

Albert G. Butzer, III

CSS Publishing Company, Inc., Lima, Ohio

TEARS OF SADNESS, TEARS OF GLADNESS

Copyright © 2001 by
CSS Publishing Company, Inc.
Lima, Ohio

All rights reserved. No part of this publication may be reproduced in any manner whatsoever without the prior permission of the publisher, except in the case of brief quotations embodied in critical articles and reviews. Inquiries should be addressed to: Permissions, CSS Publishing Company, Inc., P.O. Box 4503, Lima, Ohio 45802-4503.

Scripture quotations are from the *New Revised Standard Version of the Bible,* copyright 1989 by the Division of Christian Education of the National Council of the Churches of Christ in the USA. Used by permission.

Library of Congress Cataloging-in-Publication Data

Butzer, Albert G., 1954-
    Tears of sadness, tears of gladness : gospel sermons for Lent and Easter, cycle A / Albert G. Butzer, III.
      p. cm.
    Includes bibliographical references.
    ISBN 0-7880-1823-X (alk. paper)
    1. Lenten sermons. 2. Bible. N.T. Gospels—Sermons. I. Title.
BV4277 .B79 2001
252'.62—dc21   2001025098
                                                                                       CIP

For more information about CSS Publishing Company resources, visit our website at www.csspub.com.

ISBN 0-7880-1823-X   PRINTED IN U.S.A.

To Betsy ...

your weekly fresh-cut flowers on the study desk remind me of the grace and beauty of God's world, and reflect the grace and beauty of your own life.

Table Of Contents

Preface by John M. Buchanan	7
Ash Wednesday Lent — A Tithe Of Days Matthew 6:1-6, 16-21	11
Lent 1 Tempted In The Strong Places Of Life Matthew 4:1-11	17
Lent 2 New Eyes For The (Spiritually) Needy John 3:1-17	23
Lent 3 Drinking From The Same Cup John 4:5-42	29
Lent 4 How Should Christians Relate To Jews Today? John 9:1-41	33
Lent 5 Tears Of Sadness, Tears Of Gladness John 11:1-45	41
Passion/Palm Sunday The Cry Of The Vacant Heart Matthew 26:14—27:66	47
Maundy Thursday Receiving In Order To Give John 13:1-17, 31b-35	53

Good Friday   **59**
    Looking At Life From The Point Of View Of Death
    John 18:1—19:42

Easter   **63**
    Resurrection In A Cross-Shaped World
    John 20:1-18

Easter 2   **69**
    Doubting Thomas And His Twin
    John 20:19-31

Easter 3   **75**
    Wide-Eyed Recognition
    Luke 24:13-35

Easter 4   **81**
    Listening For The Voice Of The Good Shepherd
    John 10:1-10

Easter 5   **87**
    The Truth About Jesus
    John 14:1-14

Easter 6   **93**
    Living In Two Worlds At Once
    John 14:15-21

Ascension Of The Lord   **99**
    The Three *W*s Of The Christian Life
    Luke 24:44-53

Easter 7   **107**
    Praying For The Church
    John 17:1-11

Preface

It was English novelist P. G. Wodehouse who observed that the preaching clergyperson has an opportunity afforded to no one else, namely to speak uninterrupted for twenty or thirty minutes to a gathering of people who have come to listen. Week after week, in every community across our nation and throughout much of the world, people engage in what amounts to a counter-cultural activity. They gather in churches to worship God, to express their beliefs, to pray, to sing praises, to give their resources to support the work they believe God wants done in the world, and to listen to the words of one they have invited to be their preacher and who they have agreed not only to hear, but to compensate for his or her labors.

Those of us who do this job know both its high privilege and its awesome responsibility. I love to recall Fred Craddock's image of the people paying the preacher to go to the study for them each week, to inquire of the scriptures on their behalf, and then to bring to Sunday morning what he or she has discovered. The people of Providence Presbyterian Church in Fairfax, Virginia, have the privilege weekly of hearing the words of one who takes this responsibility very seriously and has become a classic practitioner of the art and craft of preaching.

A sermon is an event that brings together five elements:
- a biblical text, carefully studied in its context;
- the theological tradition: what classic and modern scholarship have said about the text and subject;
- the life of the world;
- the life and experience of a particular congregation;
- the faith and experience of the preacher.

The Reverend Albert G. Butzer, III, does his homework and brings these five dynamics together in sermons he offers with consistency and creativity.

His sermons are biblically based. Following the Revised Common Lectionary for Year A through Lent and Easter, the author grounds each sermon in careful study of scripture informed by the best available scholarship. Then he brings to the task the theologians, Jürgen Moltmann, Joseph Sittler, Douglas John Hall, among others. The reader and listener encounter in these sermons, in addition, the insights of some of the brightest and best current preachers: Barbara Brown Taylor, Peter Gomes, William Willimon.

Albert Butzer says this about preaching: "Sermons should speak to the real and immediate lives of the listeners and be grounded in the everyday events of their lives." This collection of Butzer's sermons accomplishes that goal admirably. Longfellow and Shakespeare and Edna St. Vincent Millay appear here but so do C. S. Lewis, Dan Wakefield, Doris Betts, and even Paul Simon. Butzer heeds Karl Barth's famous advice to the preacher to hold an open Bible in one hand and an open newspaper in the other thereby bringing to his congregation and readers the events about which they are thinking at the moment: political turmoil, international conflict, racism, homophobia, and violence in American life.

Because he is a pastor as well as a preacher, Butzer's sermons become personal and intimately relevant. His arresting anecdotes include the modern dilemma of over-busyness and life which seems out of control — expressed with familiar poignancy: "This in not how I intended to live my life." He discusses human grief, the temptation to succeed, in ways that I found helpful. And, week after week he helps his congregation and readers to put the entirety of their lives in the context of the Good News of God's saving love in Jesus Christ. These sermons represent an individual's weekly offering of his faith, experience, hope, and passion to his people. As such, they are an act of devotion. And they are an example of preaching at its most basic and most classic.

"The Christian Church is always one generation from extinction," sounds like a cliché but there is truth in it, urgent truth, in fact. Something is afoot. Old denominationalism seems less and less relevant as new Pentecostalism sweeps much of the globe. The world seems at once more secular and more spiritual. And in the middle of it all, trying to make sense of it, while telling the old story week in and week out is the preaching clergyperson. After a long period of minimizing the importance of preaching, there are signs that we are recovering a sense of the pulpit's power and potential for renewing the church and building up the body of Christ for a new millennium. There are clear signs that the church is strengthened and individual lives transformed when preaching is taken seriously.

Ever since that day the Apostle Peter stood up after the overwhelming experience of Pentecost and for the first time put the story of Jesus into words — preached a sermon — Christians have experienced the way human words become God's word and the Word made flesh in Jesus Christ becomes real and compelling in the lives of men and women and children. No one knows the mystery of it more clearly than the preacher whose words are somehow used by God. No one is more humbled by the experience than one whose hard work and love for God and hopes for the world and commitment to the congregation take the form of a weekly sermon in which the reality of God and God's love in Jesus Christ suddenly and mysteriously come into focus for people in the gathered congregation.

Thanks be to God for women and men with the courage and grace and passion to keep doing it, to offer their work and words to their people weekly. Thanks be to God for continuing to use preachers and their preaching to convey the Good News of the Gospel.

> John M. Buchanan
> Pastor, Fourth Presbyterian Church
> Chicago, Illinois

Ash Wednesday
Matthew 6:1-6, 16-21

Lent — A Tithe Of Days

Many of us feel that our lives are out of control. Hurried and hectic, frantic and frenzied — this is the way we describe the craziness of our daily lives. One woman spoke of her dilemma with words like these: "I never thought I'd be living like this. Somehow I imagined my life would be simpler, less complicated. I'm forty years old and I really should have my life together, but everything seems chaotic and out of control." Then with a sigh, she added, "This in not how I intended to live my life."[1]

Sometimes we look to modern technology to provide our salvation. But often, the very technology we depend on to simplify life does just the opposite — it complicates life. For example, the cell phone meant to give us freedom instead ties us to the office like some unseen umbilical cord. The lap top computer designed to allow us to work wherever we like, often means that we work wherever we *are*. Even e-mail, intended to speed communication, is not without its problems. A recent article wonders whether you're either rude or inept if you fail to answer a client's e-mail within thirty minutes. Sometimes, the source of our craziness is the very technology we once believed could save us.

But at other times, the chaos of life is of our own making, and we have no one to blame but ourselves. We want a nicer home with a bigger yard so we move farther out, thereby increasing our daily commute. We want our children to be well-rounded so we sign them up for scouts and soccer and school band, but what we lose is the dinner hour as we wolf down our food and then pile into the car to get to practice on time. We show up at a community meeting wanting to get involved, but grow resentful when they ask us to chair the next fund-raiser. There are only so many hours in a day, and our time is no longer our own. No wonder that woman speaks for many of us when she says in frustration, "This is not how I intended to live my life."

The Christian faith offers us a remedy for the craziness of life, and the season of Lent lies at the heart of it. Lent is the forty-day season of the church year, which extends from Ash Wednesday to the Saturday just before Easter (not counting Sundays). Lent is patterned after the forty days Jesus spent in the wilderness at the start of his public ministry, as well as after the forty years the people of Israel wandered through the wilderness until they arrived at the Promised Land. As such, Lent is a time to ponder the profound issues of life and faith, to look into the very depth of our own soul, to examine our priorities and commitments, to come to terms with our own mortality, to get in touch with the chaotic wilderness of our own life, and then resolve to begin to do things differently.

In one of his books, the noted Presbyterian minister and writer Frederick Buechner points out that the forty days of Lent correspond to approximately one tenth of each year's days.[2] In other words, Lent is something like a tithe of days. Just as people of faith set aside a tithe — one tenth of their income — for some holy use, so Lent invites us to set aside one tenth of the days of the year, to spend them on God and on God's work in the world. Buechner suggests a number of questions to ponder during Lent. Here are several: If you had to bet everything you have on whether there is a God or whether there isn't, which side would get your money and why? If you had only one last message to leave to a handful of people who are most important to you, what would it be in 25 words or less? If this were the last day of your life, what would you do with it?[3]

Lent, a tithe of days. What a fascinating way to think about this forty-day season of the church year, and what a marvelous investment opportunity. Lent begins with Ash Wednesday. How then will we spend it?

The Gospel reading from the sixth chapter of Matthew offers a model for Lenten devotion by suggesting several specific faith practices: giving alms — that is, giving to charitable causes which minister to the poor and the dispossessed, prayer, fasting, and evaluating your financial priorities. In other words, Jesus suggests several specific things *to do* to enhance our devotion.

However, if the truth be known, most of us don't need anything more to do. Our plate is already full. Life is much too chaotic as it is. We don't need anything else to cram into our already-too-busy lives. Yes, it's true, we desperately want to grow in our faith, but not if it means more work to do. We want a deep and abiding experience of the living God, but we want it the easy way with little or no effort or discipline. Leonard Sweet, the Methodist seminary professor, observes: "Wanting to be rich without working, smart without studying, and holy without giving up any vices is how one New Age critic characterizes the reigning mentality [of our day]."[4]

But experience suggests that improvement comes through practice. The piano student will spend hours working on her scales before she can master Bach. The weekend golfer will hit buckets and buckets of practice balls to knock a stroke or two off his handicap. The high school student preparing for the SATs will study and study and study some more until all of those obscure vocabulary words become familiar. Practice leads to improvement in all areas of life, including the religious life.

You notice that the emphasis here is not on "giving up" something for Lent, a form of self-denial that has much good in it. Rather, the emphasis is on "taking on" something for Lent. In a book called *Reformed Spirituality*, seminary professor Howard Rice writes:

> *It is the discipline that we take on ourselves more than the discipline of removing something from our lives that may most determine our spirituality ... a contemporary list of religious acts would probably include:*
> *1) Moral living including breaking bad habits;*
> *2) Prayer and private devotion;*
> *3) The use of devotional literature including the Bible as daily reading;*

4) *Regular church attendance;*
5) *Service to others, including both witnessing and acts of charity and love.*[5]

Many churches invite their members to practice their faith through a variety of Lenten spiritual disciplines. This Lent please consider one or more of the following faith practices: using a daily devotional booklet; learning how to sense the presence of God in the midst of your daily life through prayer and meditation; participating in a Bible study; attending church services each Sunday; contributing to a special offering like One Great Hour of Sharing; performing weekly some act of kindness and mercy for someone in need.

Think about this Lenten season as a tithe of days; you will be surprised how God can become real to you, more than you ever imagined.

Of course, the risk of taking on some Lenten practice is that we might become puffed up with the pride of our own accomplishments. There is nothing more glorious than someone whose spiritual life overflows with the love and grace of God. And there is nothing more gaudy than someone who feels the need to brag and boast about it, "to stir it and stump it and blow your own trumpet,"[6] as a phrase from a Gilbert and Sullivan opera suggests. Maybe that's why Jesus cautions us not to become spiritual showoffs. "Beware of practicing your piety before others in order to be seen by them. So," he says, "whenever you give alms, do not sound the trumpet ... and whenever you pray do not be like the hypocrites who love to be seen by others ... and whenever you fast do not look dismal so as to show others that you are fasting." No, says Jesus, when you give alms and pray and fast, do so in secret. Do it for God and do it for yourself, but please don't parade your piety in public. As Jesus suggests, "Whenever you pray, go into your room and shut the door and pray to your Father who is in secret; and your Father who sees in secret will reward you" (Matthew 6:6).

Some years ago Dan Wakefield, the novelist and journalist, wrote a wonderful spiritual memoir called *Returning*. In the preface of the book, he describes the changes that came over some of those who attended a class on the spiritual life:

I watched some of my fellow seekers grow and change, and in deep and quiet ways experience the power of healing simply through becoming closer to the spiritual element in their lives.[7]

It's a wonderful phrase: *in deep and quiet ways* their lives were changed, just as your life can be changed, as well as mine, from chaos to calm and from stress to serenity by the grace and power of God.

---

1. See Craig Dykstra and Dorothy C. Bass, "Times of Yearning, Practices of Faith" in *Practicing Our Faith*, Dorothy C. Bass, ed. (San Francisco: Jossey-Bass Publishers, 1997), p. 1.

2. Frederick Buechner, *Whistling In The Dark* (San Francisco: Harper Collins Publishers, 1993), p. 82.

3. *Ibid.*

4. Leonard I. Sweet, *Quantum Spirituality, A Postmodern Apologetic* (Dayton, Ohio: Whaleprints Publishing Company, 1991), p. 282.

5. Howard L. Rice, *Reformed Spirituality* (Louisville: Westminster/John Knox Press, 1991), p. 186.

6. Quoted in Roger L. Shinn, *The Sermon On The Mount* (New York: The Pilgrim Press, 1962), p. 9.

7. Dan Wakefield, *Returning: A Spiritual Journey* (New York: Penguin Books, 1988), p. xii.

Lent 1
Matthew 4:1-11

Tempted In The
Strong Places Of Life

In his best-selling book called *First You Have To Row a Little Boat*, Richard Bode writes about sailing with the wind, or "running down wind," as sailors sometimes speak of it. When you're running with the wind, the wind is pushing you from behind, so it's easy to be lulled into a false sense of security. Writes Bode:

> *Since my boat and I were moving at almost the same speed as the wind, I could barely feel its refreshing touch against my face. The warm sun beat down on my back. I slumped on the cockpit floorboards ... telling myself if ever I could sink into blissful indolence, this was such a time.*[1]

Suddenly without warning, Bode experienced what sailors call an accidental jibe. The wind got in behind his outstretched mainsail and threw the heavy wooden boom across the boat with such tremendous force that it crashed into a stainless steel stay, ripped a fitting from the deck and tipped the mast. Writes Bode: "Had I been sitting up on the deck, instead of down in the cockpit, my head surely would have been knocked from my neck."[2]

While his boat was being repaired, Bode had time to ponder the lesson he'd learned.

> *I was to jibe many times in my life, before I understood that going with the wind is the most dangerous course of all ... I found it deceptively easy to let myself be*

*lulled into that false sense of security that so often surrounds us when the wind is at our back.*³

The topic of this sermon is temptation, but not the usual temptations, the so-called "temptations of weakness." Let's not talk about the temptations to cheat, lie, steal, commit adultery, over-eat, or over-indulge. These are all temptations of weakness. Rather, let's ponder the so-called "temptations of strength," the challenges we face when everything is going well — when we are succeeding in life, when we have the world by the tail, when the sun is shining and the wind is at our back. These kinds of temptations are often much more subtle, much more seductive, much more demonic.

In the scripture lesson from Matthew, notice that the devil does not tempt Jesus to fail, to succumb to weakness. Just the opposite — the devil tempts Jesus to succeed! The devil seems to say:

Don't you want the common people to rally around your ministry? Just turn these stones into loaves of bread and you'll have more followers than you know what to do with. You say you want to prove to people that you're the Son of God? Then throw yourself from the top of the temple, and God will rescue you. You say you want to establish your kingdom here on earth? You say you want to rule over the nations? Well, it can all be yours, if you do just one little thing for me. You say you want to be a success, Jesus? It's as easy as one, two, three.

The devil, you see, tempts Jesus to succeed, not to fail. The devil tempts him not where he is weak but in the strong places of life.

Those of you in the business world know what I'm talking about. The greatest temptations come, not when you are performing poorly, but when you are succeeding, when you are doing one *hell* of a good job. According to college chaplain Will Willimon, that is when the boss calls you in and says, "We want to give you a bigger sales territory. We think you're going places. You've got all the right stuff."

"But I don't want a bigger sales territory," you reply. "I'm already away from home three nights a week as it is. What about my family?"

"What about your family," says the boss. "It's because of your family that we want you to take the job. You need a lot of money to support a family these days. You want to keep them happy, don't you? So take the job, take it for them!"[4]

Or let me use my own profession as an example. We clergy are most susceptible to temptation, not when the pews are empty and the church is going down the drain, but when the congregation is vital and alive and the parking lot is full. How easy to be lulled into a false sense of self, to feel that we are more important than we really are, to believe that the rules we preach for others don't apply to us. In the worst-case scenarios, such temptations can lead to clergy misconduct.

In her important though disturbing book, *Is Nothing Sacred?* Marie Fortune tells the story of the Reverend Peter Donovan. When Donovan came to First Church, he began to attract new members almost immediately. At first, the old timers were glad that Donovan was bringing in so many new members and getting them into leadership positions. But eventually a pattern began to emerge. "Donovan recruited people to *him*," writes Marie Fortune. "He elicited commitments to himself, not to the church. Many of the newcomers were more fans of Pete Donovan than members of First Church."[5] But never mind! The church was growing, the programs were flourishing, excitement was high. Yet something was not quite right. Some of the people felt manipulated. Others began to suspect that Donovan was acting inappropriately with certain women in the church. A huge split developed in the church, some fiercely loyal to Donovan, others who felt that they had been duped. In the end, he lost his job. They said it was adultery that did him in, but they were only partly right. The root of the problem was not just adultery but an abuse of the power of his pastoral position. He had taken advantage of women who were most vulnerable — one of them grieving the death of her husband, another young, naive, and starry-eyed, another recently divorced. Just as it is the psychiatrist's solemn responsibility to make sure that the patient remains on the psychiatrist's couch and never ends up in his bed, so clergy need to understand the power of their position, and honor appropriate boundaries. As you can imagine, the outcome was disastrous: the victimized women needed years of counseling to get their lives back together, the congregation was torn apart, and a dynamic pastor lost his job.

Of course, sometimes it's not individual clergy who are at fault but the institutional church itself. I own a beautiful book of reproductions of famous paintings of biblical scenes. The book contains a remarkable painting of Jesus' temptation, which is deeply disturbing for those of us who are employed by the church. In this masterpiece painted by a sixteenth century Flemish artist, the devil comes to Jesus out in the wilderness. Do you know how the devil is dressed? He is dressed in the robe of a medieval monk with rosary beads in his hand.[6] In other words, the devil is dressed up as the Church!

How many times has the Church been tempted to use its position of strength to promote not evil dressed as evil, but evil dressed as good. "Come," said the Church in the Middle Ages, "give us your money and your young men so that we can go and wage war against the Moslem infidels and reclaim the Holy City, *our* Holy City of Jerusalem." "Come," said the Church at the time of Martin Luther, "give us your indulgences and you can buy your loved ones out of purgatory." "Come on," said some parts of the Church right here in America less than 200 years ago, "if people in the Bible had slaves, then slavery must be God's will for us still." "Come on," said some parts of the Presbyterian Church just fifty years ago, "If the Bible says, 'Women should be silent in the churches' (1 Corinthians 14:34), then who are we to think of ordaining them as deacons, elders, and ministers?" How many times has the Church itself succumbed to temptations of strength?

And what can we say of those who rule the nation? One day in the nation's capital, the most powerful man in the land eyed a beautiful young woman. He summoned her, seduced her, and later tried to hide the truth. He enlisted the help of a trusted confidant who covered the whole thing over and made it look as if the leader was blameless. Did the confidant know all the facts, or did his fierce loyalty to his boss blind him to the truth? We may never know. But we do know that the leader's indiscretion did not go unnoticed, especially by God. So God sent the prophet Nathan to confront the king with his sin. They said it was adultery that caused King David to stumble, but they were only partly right. The root of the problem for the most powerful man in the land was not just adultery but an abuse of the power of his position. He took advantage of a starry-eyed young woman who didn't know how to say, "No."

This nation, the good old United States, has been experiencing some temptations of its own. As a nation, we too have been tempted in the strong places of our national life. How easy to ignore the moral indiscretions in Washington as long as the nation is strong and powerful. With military planes and warships flexing their muscle in the hot spots around the world, how convenient to remember that we are the strongest nation on the face of the earth. With the stock market soaring, interest rates low, and the national debt on the decline, how easy to say that what happens behind closed doors doesn't matter. How convenient to believe that public and private morality have nothing to do with each other. As long as our ship of state is on course with the sun shining, our sails full, and the wind at our back, how deceptively easy to be lulled into a false sense of security.

And meanwhile, says Luke's version of Jesus' temptation, "The devil departed until an opportune time" (Luke 4:13). No one knows for sure, but maybe that opportune time for the devil to return is now.

---

1. Richard Bode, *First You Have To Row A Little Boat*, (New York: Time Warner Books Publishers, 1993), pp. 62-64.

2. *Ibid.*

3. *Ibid.*

4. William Willimon, *What's Right With The Church* (San Francisco: Harper & Row, Publishers, 1985), pp. 108-109.

5. This quote and much of the information in this paragraph is taken from Marie M. Fortune, *Is Nothing Sacred?* (San Francisco: Harper Collins Publishers, 1989), quote from p. 7.

6. Juan des Flandes, "Temptation of Christ in the Wilderness" in *The Bible In Art*, Richard Muhlberger, ed. (New York: Portland House Publishers, 1990), p. 57.

Lent 2
John 3:1-17

New Eyes For The (Spiritually) Needy

Perhaps you have heard of an organization called "New Eyes for the Needy." Their mission is simple yet incredibly important. They collect old eyeglasses from people who can no longer use them, and they give them to people who need them, but can't afford to buy a new pair for themselves. "New Eyes for the Needy" — it's not only their name but describes their mission as well.

The scripture from the third chapter of the Gospel of John might well be called "New Eyes for the (Spiritually) Needy," but before we get to those new eyes, we need to understand the setting. The scripture describes a conversation between Jesus and a Jewish religious leader named Nicodemus. Nicodemus comes to talk about spiritual things and Jesus looks him straight in the eye and says, "No one can see the kingdom of God without being born from above" (John 3:3), or *born again* as those words are sometimes translated. "Born again?" asks Nicodemus. "How can anyone be born after having grown old? Can one enter a second time into the mother's womb and be born?"

The Gospel writer tells us that Nicodemus came to Jesus *by night*. And if that night suggests not only the absence of daylight but also a sort of spiritual darkness then that just about says it all. For if there is one thing for sure, it is that we mainline Protestants struggle with this idea of being born again or born from above. If I had a dollar for every church member who asked, "Do I really need to be born again?" I'd be able to retire early!

Why does this idea about being born again leave us in the dark much of the time? Undoubtedly, part of the reason is because we mainline Protestants don't talk about it very much. We don't speak of it in our worship; we don't discuss it in small group Bible studies; we have not made it a regular part of our religious vocabulary. And we have good reason not to dwell on it — the New Testament itself does not dwell on it. Do you know that the phrase "born from above" or "born again" occurs just two times in the entire New Testament and both of them are in this passage? It's hardly a New Testament-wide emphasis, is it? However, you'd never know that by talking with conservative evangelical Christians. They talk constantly about being born again. How do you reply when one of your conservative friends asks, "Have you been born again? When did it happen?" How do you feel when someone like Billy Graham the famous evangelist says on television, "No matter what your church tells you, religious ritual is not enough. It's great to be baptized; it's great to be confirmed; it's great to be a participating member of a church, but that is not enough. You must be born again"?

Like Nicodemus, we just don't get it. Like Nicodemus, we remain in the dark unable to see. And like Nicodemus, we get bogged down by biology rather than thrilled by theology. "Can I enter a second time into my mother's womb and be born?" he asks. Of course not, Jesus seems to say. We're not talking about the physical world here, but about the spiritual world, a world that is much more subtle and mysterious. It is, says Jesus, a lot like the wind. "The wind blows where it chooses, and you hear the sound of it, but you do not know where it comes from or where it goes. So it is with everyone who is born of the Spirit" (John 3:8).

People who travel to the islands of the Caribbean will tell you that the winds there blow basically from the same direction all year long. The trade winds blow all the way across the Atlantic from Africa until they reach the Caribbean. As a result, the islands are affected by winds from the East which are as predictable as the daily rising of the sun. By way of contrast, the winds on the Chesapeake Bay where I sail are much less predictable. One day they will blow down from the North, another day from the Southwest. On still another day, a sea breeze off the Atlantic will fill in from the Southeast. As a result, you never know what to expect.

The wind of the Spirit is more like the wind on the Chesapeake: subtle, mysterious, always changing, rarely the same two days in a row. It is this wind — the wind of the Spirit — which can blow into your life and mine in ways that are so subtle that you hardly notice until one day you open your eyes and begin to see things differently.

Here, for example, is a middle-aged man devoted entirely to his career. He has poured his whole life into his work. He has succeeded greatly in life and has much to show for it: a beautiful home, a couple of late model cars in the garage, a cabin in the mountains, a membership at the country club. But one day he wakes up, looks around, and realizes that all is not well. His wife who was once his best friend and most trusted confidant seems distant and uncaring. He feels like a stranger to his own children. His job title — senior vice president — which he once wore with pride like a battle ribbon on a soldier's uniform, no longer means what it once did. And then, ever so gradually he begins to change. He reaches out to his wife the way he had when they were young lovers with all of life's hopes and dreams stretching out in front of them. He rebuilds bridges with his children. He begins to laugh again, to enjoy life, to give away some of his time and energy. Those who know him wonder what's come over him. They ask him about it, but he himself is not even sure. But we know, don't we! The Spirit which is like the wind has been blowing gently, nudging him to begin to look at life in a whole new way. It is almost as if he has been born all over again.

Or here's a woman sitting in church one Sunday morning. All her life she's been told how bad she is: "You're no good. You're a failure. You're a flop. You'll never amount to anything." Not surprisingly, all these critical words have become a self-fulfilling prophecy, and she has lived her life drowning in a sea of self-doubt. But on this particular Sunday the minister says something that grabs hold of her and won't let go. Preaching about the story of creation and humanity's fall from grace, the minister points out that before there was original sin there was something like original goodness or original glory. After creating man and woman, says the minister, God said that it was good. What the minister says is not a lot, especially for someone who all her life has been told how bad she is. But it's just enough to open this woman's eyes and help her look at life and God and most especially herself in an entirely new way. Can you see what's happened? She's in the process of being born from above.

Here's a young man sitting in a high school classroom. It's career day at his former school, and he was invited back to speak to the students about his line of work. After the speech, he sits in on several of the classes. In one class, the students are studying American poetry. Under his breath he mutters, "I hated this stuff back when I went to school here. It's no different now. What a waste of time." But on this particular day the students are reading from Edwin Arlington Robinson's "Richard Cory," a poem about a fashionable and popular man, the toast of the town, who nevertheless goes home one hot summer night and puts a bullet through his head. Suddenly, the young man says to himself, "My God, I know people like Richard Cory!" And for the first time in his life the profound truths of good literature speak to him and send him off on a quest — a quest that continues to this day — to reread all of the books and poems he muddled through when he was a student. Can you see what's happening to him? He is experiencing something of a personal renaissance and discovering for the first time in his life a yearning for learning. It seems that the Spirit which is like the wind has been gently blowing him in directions he never would have chosen on his own.

Here's a Sunday school teacher, faithfully doing her duty, preparing her lessons each week, teaching the children Sunday after Sunday. Most of the time she finds the assignments to be dull and boring. But this week the curriculum calls for a field trip. The children are studying the words of Jesus where he says, "Love God and love your neighbor as yourself," and so they pay a visit to the local shelter where they help out by serving a meal to the homeless people. As the homeless poor file by in their Salvation Army clothes, carrying all of their worldly possessions in brown paper grocery bags, the teacher considers her own clothes — the latest in designer fashions — and the closet full of things she never wears, and suddenly something comes over her. Her eyes fill with tears of compassion and for the first time in her life she sees these poor homeless people, not as nameless, faceless blights in an otherwise beautiful community but as real people with real problems and concerns. Although she doesn't realize it at the time, slowly but surely she is being converted to the cause of the poor as she begins to volunteer an evening a week at the shelter.

What do all of these stories have in common? They all describe the changes that came over people who allowed the fresh winds of God to blow them in directions they might not have chosen for themselves. They all describe people who were given the chance to start over, people who were given a second chance or maybe a third or a fourth. It was, you see, as if they were born all over again.

But please notice where the initiative lies — not with the individuals themselves as if they could be born again by their own efforts. Is there any one of us who came into this world by our own efforts? Of course not! You have your mother to thank for that, as well as doctors and nurses and others. All *you* can do is look back with gratitude and then live your life in a way that honors those who gave you the gift of birth in the first place.

To be born from above is much the same. You can't make it happen on your own. No, it is much too mysterious for that — it's like the wind. Rather, it is God, who like a divine midwife gives you this gift, this chance to start all over again. Sometimes the change comes over you gradually; sometimes it can come dramatically and suddenly. But one way or another the change comes.

Most often we make this business of being born from above much too complicated. For me, it is not unlike receiving a new pair of eyes. For part of your life you have looked at the world in one way. But then, one day you begin to realize that you're looking at things differently, no longer through your own eyes but through the eyes of faith. In one of his books, the Dutch Roman Catholic priest Henri Nouwen says: "This is the great call to conversion: to look [at the world] not with the eyes of my own low self-esteem, but with the eyes of God's love."[1] What we're talking about is new eyes — new eyes for the spiritually needy. Or as

Jesus puts it to Nicodemus, "No one can *see* the kingdom of God without being born from above" (John 3:3).

It would be tempting to stop right here. After all, we have been talking about being born from above, and we have considered that idea from a number of perspectives. But the passage from John won't let us stop just yet, because, frankly, being born from above is not meant to be an end in itself. To say that you have been born again but then fail to involve this "new you" in the world around you is to miss the point. As seminary professor Leonard Sweet has written: "Conversion without immersion in the life [and mission] of Jesus Christ is a perversion of the gospel."[2]

How fascinating that a passage of scripture, which begins with a one-on-one conversation about being born from above, should conclude with what is perhaps the most beautiful statement about God's world-wide mission found anywhere in the Bible:

> *For God so loved the world that he gave his only Son, so that everyone who believes in him may not perish but may have eternal life. Indeed, God did not send the Son into the world to condemn the world, but in order that the world might be saved through him.*
> — John 3:16-17

To see the world like that — as deeply loved by God and in the process of being saved — is to join forces with Christ in this great work of redemption. For most of us, that will mean looking at the world with new eyes. For as Jesus reminds us, "No one can see the kingdom of God without being born from above."

---

1. Henri J. M. Nouwen, *The Return Of The Prodigal Son* (New York: Doubleday Publishing Group, 1992), p. 99.

2. Leonard Sweet, *A Cup Of Coffee At The Soul Café* (Nashville: Broadman & Holman Publishers, 1998), p. 155.

Lent 3
John 4:5-42

Drinking From The Same Cup

Hate-filled prejudice is, unfortunately, alive and well in our world today. Recall, for example, the gruesome story about James Byrd from Jasper, Texas. Late one night Byrd, an African American, was hitchhiking along the road when three white men in a pick-up truck stopped to give him a ride. They drove him to the woods outside of town where they beat him, chained him by the ankles, and then dragged him behind their truck for three miles until his head and right arm were torn off by the jagged edge of a roadside culvert. One of the three men, John William King, a self-proclaimed white supremacist who has racist tattoos covering his body, showed no remorse when sentenced to die for his crime. In fact, he and his accomplices even invoked the name of God in defending their actions.

Or consider another hate crime, this one involving a young man named Matthew Shepard. Shepard, you may recall, was a homosexual college student, who because he was gay was pistol-whipped, robbed, tied to a fence in rural Wyoming, and left out in the cold to die. At his funeral, which was held in the family's Episcopal church, Shepard was praised as a "gentle spirit." But just outside the church, protesters, many of them calling themselves Christians, were carrying signs and banners with messages that were anything but gentle. "God hates fags," said one banner. "No tears for queers," said another. "Fag Matt in Hell" said another. Ironically, there was another sign outside the church the day of Shepard's funeral, the message on the church's signboard, which quoted the words of Jesus, "Love thy neighbor." Even those who object to homosexual behavior would find it hard to support any anti-gay protest that was so cold and callous, and so contrary to the words of Jesus, "Love thy neighbor."

Speaking of Jesus, we meet him in today's Gospel reading sitting by a well in Samaria. At first glance the story about Jesus and the woman at the well appears to be a simple story about faith. Here is this woman who comes to draw water from the well. Jesus is sitting there. He's thirsty from his travels and the heat of the day; he asks for a drink. They get to talking. He tells her about a special spiritual sustenance called "living water." They speak about worship. She asks about the Messiah; he replies, "I am he." Then she finds her friends, invites them to meet Jesus, and wonders out loud, "He can't be the Messiah, can he?" (John 4:29). Later many of those friends believe because of the woman's testimony. They say, "We know that this is truly the Savior of the world" (John 4:42). At first glance, this seems to be just a simple story about faith. And, of course, at one level it is.

But when we look more closely, we find that the story also has a deeper, more profound dimension as well. Please notice several particular details of the story. First of all, notice that the person with whom Jesus spoke was a *woman*. Even the disciples weren't sure why he would speak to a woman, although, as John tells us, they were afraid to ask, "Why are you speaking with her?" (John 4:27). Rabbis, it seems, did their best to avoid speaking to women in public.[1] Didn't this rabbi named Jesus know any better?

Secondly, notice that this woman was not just any woman, she was a *Samaritan*. For the Jews, the Samaritans weren't quite as "foreign" as the Gentiles were. Then again, they weren't "full-fledged members of the household of Israel" either.[2] They were religious and cultural outsiders whom Jews regarded with a fair measure of suspicion and distrust. This distrust was so widespread that the woman herself is startled by Jesus' initiative. She says to him, "How is it that you, a Jew, ask a drink of me, a woman of Samaria?" (John 4:9).

Thirdly, notice the preface to the story. In the opening verses of the chapter, John wants us to know that Jesus "had to go through Samaria" (John 4:4). As Professor Fred Craddock observes:

> *To say that Jesus "had to pass through Samaria" is clearly not a statement about historical or geographical necessity. Jesus' obligation to pass through Samaria is a theological statement, consistent with "for God so loved the world."*[3]

In other words, Jesus' mission, as John understood it, was not just "to the lost sheep of the house of Israel" (see Matthew 10:6), but to the whole world, even to cultural and social outsiders like the people of Samaria.

Fourthly, notice the *time of day* that the woman came to the well. Typically, people went to the well in the morning or in the evening to avoid the heat of the noon time sun. Why, then, did this woman go at noon? Maybe because she was trying to avoid something worse than the noontime heat. Maybe she wanted to avoid the burning glances of those from the town who had shunned her, because she had had five previous husbands and the man with whom she was now living was not her husband.[4] Such a lifestyle would provide grist for the gossip mill in her day as well as our own. So she went to the well at noon to avoid the townspeople who were scandalized by her lifestyle.

Do you get the sense that there is more going on in this story than at first meets the eye? For here at the well we meet this Samaritan woman and this Jewish rabbi as different from each other as James Byrd was from his racist killer, as different as Matthew Shepard was from those anti-gay protesters. Everything we know about human relations suggests that these two at the well will ignore each another at best, or even worse, taunt or demean one another. How incredibly surprising, therefore, when Jesus breaks down all the barriers of race and gender and moral superiority by making a simple request: "Give me a drink," says Jesus. But the woman protests:

> *You want me to give a drink to you? Do you know what you're asking? Don't you realize that for years your people and mine have drunk from different water fountains, eaten in separate restaurants, sat at different ends of the bus? How is it that you, a Jew, ask a drink of me,*

a woman of Samaria? We're not supposed to drink from the same cup, you know. It's against the rules. It goes against the grain of our society. Don't you know what you're asking?

But, of course, he did know what he was asking. He knew precisely what he was doing. By reaching out to this foreign woman of questionable morality, this outsider in her own world, Jesus was demonstrating the amazing grace of God. He did that often in his ministry. By "eating [and drinking] with outcasts, forgiving sinners, and calling all to repent and believe the gospel,"[5] Jesus earned the wrath of those who wanted to preserve the status quo. But by breaking down the barriers of hatred and prejudice, he shows us just how broad and deep and profound is the unconditional love of God.

Sadly, for some 2,000 years now, the Church — the Church which bears his name, the name of *Christ*-ian — has often fallen short of his example.

---

1. Raymond E. Brown, *The Gospel According To John* in the Anchor Bible Series (Garden City, NY: Doubleday & Company, Inc., 1966), p. 173.

2. See "Samaritans" in *The Interpreter's Dictionary Of The Bible* (Nashville: Abingdon Press, 1962), Volume 4, p. 191.

3. Fred B. Craddock, *John* in Knox Preaching Guides (Atlanta: John Knox Press, 1982), p. 35.

4. See Brown, p. 171, which suggests that "Jews were allowed only three marriages. If the same standard was applied among the Samaritans, then the woman's life had been markedly immoral."

5. From "A Brief Statement of Faith" in *The Book Of Confessions* (Louisville: Published by the Office of the General Assembly of the Presbyterian Church USA, 1994), 10.16-18.

**Lent 4
John 9:1-41**

How Should Christians Relate To Jews Today?

How should Christians relate to Jews in today's world? That's a question all of us should ponder. Consider a true story about the relationship between a Presbyterian minister and a Jewish rabbi. The minister was my grandfather, Dr. Albert G. Butzer; the rabbi was my grandfather's friend and colleague, Dr. Joseph Fink. The two men served neighboring congregations in Buffalo, New York, from the years prior to World War II until the 1960s. One day my grandfather received the tragic news that Temple Beth Zion had caught fire. He climbed in his car and rushed to the temple, arriving while the flames were still burning. The damage to the temple was severe; it had been all but destroyed. My grandfather found Dr. Fink at the scene and offered the sanctuary of Westminster Church as the place where the Jewish congregation could worship until they were able to rebuild. The members of the temple accepted the offer and worshiped at Westminster while their new temple was being built. Many years later, long after both men were dead and gone, the temple returned the favor and offered its sanctuary to the Presbyterians while their church was being renovated.

These same two men jointly officiated at a number of Jewish-Christian weddings long before such ceremonies were as common as they are today. But most significant of all, Dr. Fink and my grandfather had a "gentleman's bet" which said that the one who lived longer would officiate at the funeral for the other! True to their agreement, when Dr. Fink died, my grandfather played a major role in the funeral at the temple for his dear clergy colleague. All across the years their deep and abiding friendship demonstrated much of what is possible in relationships between Christians and Jews.

Unfortunately, not all Judeo-Christian relationships are so amicable. In his best-selling book about the Bible called *The Good Book*, Peter Gomes, minister of the Memorial Church at Harvard University, tells about a college student who came to see him. It was the day after the University Choir had performed Bach's *St. John's Passion* on Good Friday evening. When the young woman arrived at Dr. Gomes' office she was in tears, and the tears were not tears of joy. According to Gomes, the student's dilemma was that she loved the music of Bach. The Good Friday performance had been "the most demanding and satisfying aesthetic experience of her young life."[1] Yet, at the same time, the performance had torn her apart, because she was Jewish and she knew the German language in which Bach wrote *St. John's Passion*. While the music was beautiful, the words were filled with anti-Jewish sentiment. Professor Gomes noted that while the woman acknowledged the beauty of the music and the genius of Bach, her existential self said:

> *This text is against me and my people, and combined they represent everything horrid and hateful that has ever happened to any Jew at the hands of any Christian. How can this be good music or God's music? How dare I participate in it, much less enjoy it?*[2]

Shortly after the conversation with the young woman, Gomes asked the choir director why the performance of the *Passion* had been given in German rather than in English. The choirmaster replied, "In German it is less harsh; we can have much of the beauty without most of the pain." "That pain," says Gomes, "was not the suffering of Jesus. It was rather the pain that Christians, in the name of that suffering Jesus, have imposed upon the Jews."[3]

There is no book of the Bible more responsible for much of the anti-Jewish rhetoric than the Gospel of John. Ironically, the Gospel of John gives us some of the most hauntingly beautiful words in the New Testament:

> *For God so loved the world that he gave his only Son, so that everyone who believes in him may not perish but may have eternal life.* — John 3:16

> *I am the resurrection and the life. Those who believe in me, even though they die, will live, and everyone who lives and believes in me will never die.*
> — John 11:25-26

> *Do not let your hearts be troubled. Believe in God, believe also in me. In my Father's house there are many dwelling places. If it were not so, would I have told you that I go to prepare a place for you? And if I go and prepare a place for you, I will come again and will take you to myself, so that where I am, there you may be also.* — John 14:1-3

But this same Gospel also gives us some of the most haunting anti-Jewish words in the Bible:

> *The man went away and told the Jews that it was Jesus who had made him well. Therefore the Jews started persecuting Jesus, because he was doing such things on the sabbath.* — John 5:15-16

> *For this reason the Jews were seeking all the more to kill him, because he was not only breaking the sabbath, but was also calling God his own Father, thereby making himself equal to God.* — John 5:18

> *The Jews took up stones again to stone him.*
> — John 10:31

> *When it was evening on that day, the first day of the week, and the doors of the house where the disciples had met were locked for fear of the Jews, Jesus came and stood among them and said, "Peace be with you."*
> — John 20:19

Nowhere is the tension between Jesus and the Jews more intense in John's Gospel than in the story about the man who had been blind from birth. Jesus heals the man of his blindness — that much is obvious. But the healing takes only the first seven verses of the chapter; the rest of the chapter concerns the *controversy* that surrounds the healing. Listen between the lines to some of that tension:

> *So for the second time [the Pharisees] called the man who had been blind, and they said to him, "Give glory to God! We know that this man is a sinner." He answered, "I do not know whether he is a sinner. One thing I do know, that though I was blind, now I see." They said to him, "What did he do to you? How did he open your eyes?" He answered them, "I have told you already, and you would not listen. Why do you want to hear it again? Do you also want to become his disciples?" Then they reviled him, saying, "You are his disciple, but we are disciples of Moses. We know that God has spoken to Moses, but as for this man, we do not know where he comes from." The man answered, "Here is an astonishing thing! You do not know where he comes from, and yet he opened my eyes. We know that God does not listen to sinners, but he does listen to one who worships him and obeys his will. Never since the world began has it been heard that anyone opened the eyes of a person born blind. If this man were not from God, he could do nothing." They answered him, "You were born entirely in sins, and are you trying to teach us?" And they drove him out.*
> — John 9:24-34

How are we to make sense of this? How are we to understand the bitter rivalry John describes between Jesus and "the Jews"? One way, of course, is to accept the tension at face value. It was *the Jews* who persecuted Jesus. It was *the Jews* who plotted to kill him. It was *the Jews* who took up stones against him. It was *the Jews* who demanded his crucifixion. With an attitude like that, is it any wonder why Judeo-Christian relationships have been so strained over the years?

But there is another way to interpret these verses — to get beneath all of the anti-Jewish rhetoric and try to understand the reason behind it. Some biblical scholars believe that the early Christians were being thrown out of the synagogue because they believed in Jesus. Since many of those early Christians had been Jews first, it must have been a painful time in which even family members became divided against each other. In fact, we catch a glimpse of this threat of excommunication in the part of the scripture that deals with the parents of the blind man. The Pharisees say to the parents: "Is this your son, who you say was born blind? How then does he now see?" The parents reply, "We know that this is our son, and that he was born blind; but we do not know how it is that now he sees, nor do we know who opened his eyes. Ask him; he is of age. He will speak for himself" (John 9:19-21). "The parents said this," writes John, "because they were afraid of the Jews; for the Jews had already agreed that anyone who confessed Jesus to be the Messiah would be put out of the synagogue" (John 9:22).

Can you see how much of the anti-Jewish rhetoric in John's Gospel is fueled by this threat of excommunication? Can you see why we need to be careful not to let a family-like feud in one ancient congregation become a universal principal for hatred between Christians and Jews? Remember that in the heat of an argument, family members will often say things to one another that they don't really mean. The Gospel of John is full of that kind of heated exchange. How then should Christians relate to Jews today?

For one thing, we should remember what is obvious — Jesus was a Jew, and without the Judaism from which Christianity grew, there would be no Church today. In one of his books John Shelby Spong, who served as the Episcopal Bishop of Newark, tells about a Moslem child he met at the airport in Tel Aviv. Spong was dressed in his clerical collar with a bishop's cross around his neck. At the center of the cross was the word YHWH, the Hebrew word for LORD. Spong says that he designed the cross intentionally to affirm the Jewishness of Jesus. On seeing the cross around the bishop's neck, the Moslem child asked Spong why it had Jewish writing on it. The bishop replied, "That is my way of reminding people that the Jesus we Christians worship was Jewish and was a gift of Judaism to the world." The child looked puzzled. "Jesus was Jewish?" she asked. "I thought Jesus was Catholic."[4]

For another thing, we Christians will want to engage Jewish people in religious dialogue rather than shy away from it. Why? Because most often truth is found in the midst of dialogue. The German Christian theologian, Jürgen Moltmann, whose life and work were forever affected by the Nazi Holocaust of the Jews, offers a way that such a dialogue can proceed. He writes:

> *Today, Jewish-Christian dialogue inspires us to formulate what we think about Christ afresh. It does not constrain us to give up our Christian identity, for then the Jews would have no partner in the dialogue.*[5]

Moltmann goes on to suggest that we Christians should neither retract nor reduce our belief in Jesus, the Christ [or Messiah] of God, in order to make our belief conform to the Jewish faith in God. For then, says Moltmann:

> *This Christian faith would cease to have any interest for Jews, and would have nothing more to say to them. But it does constrain us to see Jesus in a new way ... we have to see him with the eyes of the Jews too, in dialogue.*[6]

When it comes to the Messiah, can Jews and Christians acknowledge that we have more in common than sometimes we think? For example, both of us are waiting for a messiah. Jews wait for their messiah who will come to earth, set things right, and establish God's reign here on earth. We Christians wait for our messiah to *return* to earth at the end of time, set things right, and establish God's reign here on earth. Both Christians and Jews are people who wait in faith and in hope for God to act; both of us believe in the promise of the messiah. Maybe we do have more in common than we sometimes think; and maybe that common thread of belief is enough to begin a dialogue which might put an end to years of bitter, hostile relations between our peoples.

We began with a story about a Presbyterian minister and a Jewish rabbi. Let's conclude with a story about a rabbi and a Catholic priest. Their names are Marc Gellman and Thomas Hartman, and together they are known as "The God Squad." They host a nationally syndicated weekly cable television show and have also appeared on *Good Morning America*. While their purpose is to discuss religious issues in everyday life, the subtle message they convey is that Jews and Christians can, in fact, respect each other, work together, and maintain their unique identities. Our common prayer is that their number will increase.

---

1. Peter J. Gomes, *The Good Book* (New York: William Morrow and Company, Inc., 1996), p. 102.

2. *Ibid.*, p. 103.

3. *Ibid.*

4. John Shelby Spong, *Rescuing The Bible From Fundamentalism* (San Francisco: Harper San Francisco Publishers, 1991), p. 190.

5. Jürgen Moltmann, *Jesus Christ For Today's World* (Minneapolis: Fortress Press, 1994), p. 109.

6. *Ibid.*

**Lent 5
John 11:1-45**

Tears Of Sadness, Tears of Gladness

This morning let's consider together what is often called the shortest verse in the Bible: "Jesus wept." Even though it's a bit longer in the *New Revised Standard Version* from which we just read, it's still a very short verse. But even more to the point, it is a very important verse. Jesus wept.

The Gospels tell us that Jesus wept on just one other occasion. According to Luke's Gospel, Jesus wept over the city of Jerusalem. Presumably, he wept because that city, like so many of our cities today — cities like Chicago and New York and Washington — was filled with people unwilling to embrace the reign of God which Christ came to inaugurate. So he wept over the city. Here in John's Gospel the circumstances are different. After learning of the death of Lazarus, Jesus began to weep. The question I want to invite you to ponder this morning is *why* — why did Jesus begin to weep?

Part of the reason Jesus wept may have been simply because Lazarus was his friend. That's what those standing near the tomb thought. They looked at Jesus, saw him crying and said, "See how Jesus loved him" (John 11:36). Don't you wonder how Jesus felt when he first received word that his friend Lazarus was ill to the point of death? It's a hard word to hear when the doctor says to you, "I'm sorry, but there's nothing more we can do." It's a hard word to hear when they say to you, "I'm sorry, but your loved one has at most a few months left to live." It's a hard word to hear when you learn that a friend has cancer, that another friend has been diagnosed with AIDS.

When Jesus arrives in Bethany, Martha, the sister of Lazarus, meets Jesus and says to him, "Lord, if you had been here, my brother would not have died" (John 11:21). Later, their sister, Mary, comes out and says the very same thing, "Lord, if you had been here my brother would not have died" (John 11:32). When Jesus asks, "Where have you laid him?" they say to him, "Come and see." Then, when faced with the reality of Lazarus' death, Jesus begins to weep.

Perhaps Jesus wept, even as we all weep, because he felt that a part of him had died as well. Don't you suppose that he had an emptiness deep inside, a hole in his soul, which would not soon be healed? How hard it is to hear the word that a loved one has died: hard even to go to sleep at night, you cry and cry and cry some more, until your pillow is soaked with tears and until finally you cry yourself to sleep. It's hard to hear that a loved one has died, hard even, says this scripture, for the Son of God.

For, you see, Lazarus and Jesus were friends. In fact, as one author suggests, Lazarus may have been the only friend Jesus had who was not primarily a disciple, but just a friend. "Someone Jesus didn't have to be the messiah with but could just be himself with, someone to have a drink with once in a while,"[1] someone to go for a walk with around town, someone to let his hair down with, someone just to be himself with. Lazarus and Jesus were friends, and this is part of the reason why Jesus began to weep when he learned that Lazarus was dead.

Something that the crowd asks hints at another part of the reason Jesus wept. They asked, "Could not he who opened the eyes of the blind man have kept this man from dying?" (John 11:37). The simple answer to that question is *No*! Not even Jesus, the Messiah, the Savior of the world, could keep his friend from dying, for sooner or later death comes to each of us. No matter how much we avoid it, no matter how much we evade it, no matter how many medical miracles our doctors perform to prolong our life, sooner or later death comes to us all.

Of course, some people like to say, "Yes, but it's different for Christians — for Christians there is no death." But that's nonsense. It's simply not true. Try to tell that to the widower who has just lost a spouse of 47 years. Tell it to the family in which a child has died. Tell it to anyone who has lost a loved one — that there is no death — and they will look at you as if you're crazy.

Death has a certain finality to it, which we simply must acknowledge and admit. Do you remember the famous scene at the end of Shakespeare's *King Lear*, where Lear carries his dear Cordelia into the room, knowing that she is dead, but hoping against hope that she is not? He holds a little mirror up to her mouth and says: "If that her breath will mist or stain the stone, why then she lives." But in the end, the finality of her death hits home and the king says, "Why should a dog, a horse, a rat have life, And thou no breath at all? Thou'lt come no more, Never, never, never, never, never."[2]

Never ... never again to hear to voice of your loved one. Do you remember these beautiful though painful lines from Longfellow's "The Village Blacksmith"?

> *He goes on Sunday to the church,*
> *And sits among his boys;*
> *He hears the parson pray and preach,*
> *He hears his daughter's voice,*
> *Singing in the village choir,*
> *And it makes his heart rejoice.*
>
> *It sounds to him like her mother's voice,*
> *Singing in Paradise!*
> *He needs must think of her once more,*
> *How in the grave she lies;*
> *And with his hard, rough hand he wipes*
> *A tear out of his eyes.*[3]

Never ... never again to observe your loved one doing those little things that always endeared him or her to you. Joseph Sittler, who used to teach theology at the University of Chicago, was once talking to a woman who had lost her husband. She told him how hard it was particularly late in the afternoon when she would sit in the window and watch for him to come around the corner with the evening newspaper. She said:

> *He always stopped just where he thought I couldn't see him and knocked out his pipe. He knew I didn't want him to smoke so much, although I kept sewing up the burnt holes in his coat pockets. That time of day is the hardest to get through, because I know he won't come around that corner anymore.*[4]

There is certain finality to death that we simply must acknowledge, the finality that Jesus must have felt when he learned his friend Lazarus was dead. No wonder that Jesus began to weep.

May I suggest another reason why Jesus may have wept at the tomb of Lazarus? This reason may not be obvious when you read the eleventh chapter of John, but it becomes obvious when you view the Gospel of John as a whole. For in some symbolic way the death of Lazarus is a prelude to Jesus' own death. In one of his books, Fred Craddock points to the similarities between the death of Lazarus and the death of Jesus. In both of them:

> *Jesus is troubled and weeping.*
> *He cries out with a loud voice.*
> *There is a tomb not far from Jerusalem.*
> *The tomb is a large cave with a stone across the front of it.*
> *The stone is rolled back.*
> *There is the mention of grave clothes.*[5]

What are we talking about here, the death of Lazarus or the death of Jesus? The similarities are striking. Through these similarities, John may be making an important theological point — namely, for Lazarus to come out of the tomb, Jesus must enter a tomb; for Lazarus to live, Jesus must die; for Lazarus to believe that Jesus is the resurrection and the life, Jesus must first go to the cross. At the tomb of Lazarus, Jesus comes face to face with the impending reality of his *own* death. No wonder that Jesus, standing outside the tomb, began to weep.

Yet, here is the Good News. Here is our Christian belief in life after death. On another occasion in John's Gospel Jesus says, "Very truly, I tell you, unless a grain of wheat falls to the earth and dies, it remains just a single grain; but if it dies, it bears much fruit" (John 12:24). It's as simple as this — if Jesus had not died on the cross and then been raised from the dead, there would be no truth to his words, "I am the resurrection and the life. Those who believe in me even though they die will live, and everyone who lives and believes in me will never die" (John 11:25). But since he did die, even as we all must, and since God raised him from the dead, then there is eternal life for us as well.

By the way, this eternal life is not just what will happen in the hereafter, but also by the grace of God what can happen in the here and now. As Frederick Buechner has written, "We think of eternal life as what happens when life ends. We would do better to think of it as what happens when life begins."[6] Have you ever thought of eternal life like that — not just what happens when life ends, but also what happens when you begin a whole new life living in the gracious presence of God through Jesus Christ?

Edmund Steimle, a Lutheran minister, points to something as simple as the alarm clock going off in the morning and asks:

> *For what is this process of waking up in the morning ... to face the new day? Why, it's a miracle — like rising from the dead. A new day. None like it ever before, and none like it will ever follow. It's a daily act of God's creation.*[7]

Some of you may know the name Rufus Jones. He was an American Quaker theologian, and years ago Rufus Jones went to England to preach and to lecture. While he was in England, his son back here in America died. There were no jet planes in those days to whisk him back to America in time for his son's funeral, so Rufus Jones remained in England, while his son was being buried in America. On the day of his funeral, his friends marveled at his serenity and his grace, and they told him so. And Rufus Jones replied, "All our lives my son and I have loved Jesus Christ and been loved by him. And if this has been true in this life, will it not be true even more in the life to come?"[8]

Yes, Jesus wept, and we can all weep with him because death is real and it is personal and it is painful. But at some point our tears of sadness are transformed into tears of gladness, because of him, because of Christ. Thanks be to God who gives us this victory, even this victory over death!

---

1. Frederick Buechner, *Telling The Truth* (San Francisco: Harper and Row, Publishers, 1977), p. 37.

2. William Shakespeare *Four Tragedies*, "King Lear" Act V, Scene 3 (New York: Penguin Books, 1994), p. 782.

3. Henry Wadsworth Longfellow, *Favorite Poems*, "The Village Blacksmith" (New York: Dover Publications, Inc., 1992), p. 8.

4. Joseph Sittler, *Gravity And Grace* (Minneapolis: Augsburg Publishing House, 1986), pp. 125-126.

5. Fred B. Craddock, *John* in the Knox Preaching Guides, John H. Hayes, ed. (Atlanta: John Knox Press, 1982), p. 87.

6. Frederick Buechner, quoted in a Lenten booklet "From Death to Life" (St. Louis: Creative Communications, 1991), p. 16.

7. Edmund A. Steimle, *God The Stranger* (Philadelphia: Fortress Press, 1979), p. 32.

8. Quoted in R. Maurice Boyd, *Permit Me Voyage* (Burlington, Ontario: Welch Publishing Company, Inc., 1989), p. 152.

Passion/Palm Sunday
Matthew 26:14—27:66

The Cry Of The Vacant Heart

One of the harsh realities of the life of faith is feeling abandoned by God. Sooner or later most of us will experience what college chaplain Will Willimon once called "vacant places of the heart when God seems far away, remote."[1] We often hear people say, "I come to church to celebrate the presence of God in my life," which is true for many people much of the time. But if we listen carefully we will hear others say:

> *I come to church to try to find what's missing in my life.*
> *I come hoping that Someone will shed some light on my darkness.*
> *I come so that Someone will fill my emptiness.*
> *I come to church wanting Someone to answer all my doubts and questions.*

Haven't you ever experienced one of those vacant places of the heart? Haven't you ever felt abandoned by God? Haven't you ever wanted to cry out, "Why, God, why?"

Even Jesus felt God's absence. As strange as it may seem, God's own Son experienced one of those vacant places of the heart, because he was wrapped in the garment of our humanity. As such, he experienced abandonment just as we all do. Do you remember the way that Matthew describes the day of Jesus' crucifixion? "From noon on, darkness came over the whole land until three o'clock in the afternoon. And about three o'clock, Jesus cried with a loud voice, *Eli, Eli, lema sabachthani*? that is, 'My God, my God, why have you forsaken me?' " (Matthew 27:45-46).

Can you see the droplets of blood oozing from that crown of thorns that had been thrust down upon his head? Can you see the blood flowing down his face, the nails in his hands and feet, the wound in his side? Can you see the weak and vacant look in his eyes as he gazes into the heavens and cries out, "Why?" But there is something else that should catch our eye on that hill outside Jerusalem: the *darkness*. Not just the cross, not just the crucified Christ, not even the two thieves who were put to death with him, one on the right and one on the left. But the darkness. That is what surprises us; that's what we don't expect to see — the darkness. Remember, Matthew tells us that it's noon, the brightest time of day, the time when the sun is highest in the sky. And yet, writes Matthew, "From noon on, darkness came over the whole land" (Matthew 27:45).

Can you see that darkness? Can you sense it? Not only the darkness that engulfed Jesus around and about, but also the darkness he felt inside as well as out, the darkness of feeling abandoned by God? Scott Peck, the popular psychiatrist, says that as children one of our first and greatest fears is the fear of being abandoned. We feel it when we are but six months old, and it scares us as much as does the fear of death.[2] No matter how often our parents try to reassure us, no matter how often they say, "Don't worry, Mommy and Daddy are here; don't worry, Mommy and Daddy won't leave you," we continue to be afraid. If we are afraid of being abandoned by our earthly parents, how much more are we afraid of being abandoned by God the Father, our heavenly Parent? No wonder Jesus cried out from the darkness of his cross, "My God, my God, why have you forsaken me?"

Many of us have experienced this feeling of being abandoned by God: the young child who watches her parents divorce and then late at night cries out from the darkness of her bedroom, "My God, my God, why?"; the inner city family whose eleven-year-old boy is caught in the crossfire while riding his new bicycle on his birthday; the family who stand by an open grave as their loved one, killed by a drunk driver, is lowered into the ground; the business person who has poured his whole life into his work, loyal to the same company for years, only to be let go in the twilight of his career. And so we cry out, even as Jesus cried out from the cross, "My God, my God, why have you forsaken me?"

Thoughtful people of faith have been trying to make sense of this question for as long as there have been people of faith. But the answers they offer never seem satisfactory, never quite fill the vacant heart's cry of "why?" C. S. Lewis was a popular Christian author, and several years ago they made a movie of his life called *Shadowlands*. Early in his career, Lewis thought he had it all figured out. He went around explaining pain and suffering as if they were nothing more complicated than two plus two equals four. "Suffering is God's megaphone," he said, "God's way of rousing a deaf world. It's God's way of driving us out of the nursery and helping us to grow up." But then Lewis met a woman and fell in love. Later, when she came down with cancer, for the first time in his adult life Lewis came face to face with the problem of pain. "If you love someone," he said, "you don't want her to suffer. You can't bear it. You want to take that suffering onto yourself. If I feel like that, then why doesn't God?" Where before Lewis had handed out answers like a millionaire hands out dollar bills on the street corner, now he had only questions. He grew sick of people with pietistic answers to complex questions and hated himself for having been one of them. In the end, he concluded, there were no answers, at least no slick and simple answers, just painful and profound questions. "This earthly life of ours," he said, "is but a pale precursor of the blessed life to come, a shadowland," is what he came to call it.[3]

Hanging on the cross, Jesus experienced a shadowland of his own and cried out for an answer to the unanswerable question — Why? But in addition to asking, "Why?" he may have been doing something else as well. He may have been quoting from the Book of Psalms, the hymnal of the ancient Hebrew people. Do you find that strange, that in this moment of anguish and abandonment, Jesus would quote from a hymn? Yet that, it seems, is precisely what he does — he quotes from Psalm 22. Even though it is a hymn that begins in anguish, it ends in affirmation. Even though it begins with a puzzling, "Why?" it ends in praise. Consider just a few of the psalm's concluding lines:

> *I will tell of your name to my brothers and sisters; in the midst of the congregation I will praise you ... All the ends of the earth shall remember and turn to the LORD; and all the families of the nations shall worship before him. For dominion belongs to the LORD, and he rules over the nations.* — Psalm 22:22, 27-28

Dominion belongs to the Lord, sings the psalmist. Dominion — that means authority, control, power, supremacy. When I was a boy growing up in Buffalo, my family had a little cottage in Canada, just across the border. Although Canada had been an independent country since 1931, evidence of British dominion was still everywhere. For example, we drove on a highway known as the QEW, the Queen Elizabeth Way; we spent money that pictured the Queen on the paper currency; we even bought our groceries in a supermarket chain called *Dominion*. Evidence of Britain's dominion over Canada was everywhere, even years after independence.

Don't you wish God's dominion were as obvious as that? But it's not. I'd like to tell you that it is, but it's not, for God's dominion is not a matter of objective proof. Rather, it is a matter of faith and of trust.

A generation ago Peter Marshall was the minister of the New York Avenue Presbyterian Church in Washington, D.C. At the same time he served as the Chaplain to the Senate. Tragically, he died of a heart attack in his early forties. About a week before his death, Peter and his wife Catherine were visiting friends in a nearby city. They spent the night in the guestroom, where there were twin beds. Late that evening, after they'd gone to bed and turned out the lights, long after the house was quiet, Catherine stretched out a hand toward Peter's bed and felt Peter's hand reaching out in the darkness toward hers. "How did you know my hand was there?" he whispered. She replied, "I don't know. I just *knew*."[4]

God's dominion is something similar. We can't prove it; we just know. A seminary professor once put it like this: "When you're driving your car at night, you can't see any farther than the headlights. But you can make the whole trip that way if you just trust that the road continues."[5]

At the end of World War II, some American soldiers found some words scrawled on the basement wall of a home in Germany. A Jewish family had owned the home. We can imagine them huddled in the basement in fear, wondering how God could allow the Nazis to work their horrors against them and their people. Can't you imagine them cowering in fear and crying out in anguish, "My God, my God, why?" Yet, on the basement wall they had etched a Star of David and next to the star one of them had written these words:

> *I believe in the sun even when it is not shining.*
> *I believe in love even when I do not feel it.*
> *I believe in God even when God is silent.*[6]

That's a belief in God's dominion.

Prior to his death, Winston Churchill left instructions that "Taps" should be played at his funeral. "Taps," the bugler's solemn and somber song, which seems to ask the question, Why? Why death? Why now? Why this dear person? But Churchill had arranged one final surprise. For as soon as that bugler finished playing "Taps," another bugler began to play. Do you know what he played? "Reveille," the song which wakes us from our deathlike sleep to begin again a new day. It was Churchill's way of affirming God's dominion, even God's dominion over death.

This is why we so often speak of faith as a journey, because it implies movement, the same kind of movement we find in Psalm 22. To be able to move from anguish to affirmation, from a puzzling "Why?" to a song of praise is one of the greatest trips we will ever make. "I will tell of your name to my brothers and sisters," sings the psalmist. "In the midst of the congregation I will praise you" (Psalm 22:22).

---

1. William H. Willimon, *With Glad And Generous Hearts* (Nashville: The Upper Room Press, 1986), p. 54.

2. M. Scott Peck, *The Road Less Traveled* (New York: Touchstone Books, 1978), p. 25.

3. Leonore Fleischer, *Shadowlands*, based on the screenplay by William Nicholson (New York: Signet Books, 1993), pp. 36, 185, 256, 258.

4. Catherine Marshall, *To Live Again* (New York: McGraw-Hill Book Company, Inc., 1957), p. 106.

5. Quoted by Fred B. Craddock in a lecture at the Presbyterian Church Head of Staff Conference, Orlando, Florida, February 1997.

6. Quoted in W. Frank Harrington, *Seeking A Living Faith* (Lima, Ohio: CSS Publishing Company, Inc., 1988), p. 49.

Maundy Thursday
John 13:1-17, 31b-35

Receiving In Order To Give

According to the Apostle Paul, Jesus once said, "It is more blessed to give than to receive" (Acts 20:35). Not surprisingly, all across the years the Church has agreed! What is the weekly offering but an opportunity for people to give rather than to receive? What are annual stewardship drives and special offerings like One Great Hour Of Sharing but opportunities to give rather than to receive? What are invitations to sing in the choir, teach in the Sunday school, volunteer at the soup kitchen, and go off on mission trips to far-away places like Mexico but opportunities to give rather than to receive? "It is more blessed to give than to receive," said Jesus, and all across the years the Church has nodded in agreement.

Clearly, the reading from the thirteenth chapter of John contains a strong emphasis on giving. Jesus gets up from the table, takes off his outer robe, grabs a towel and a basin of water, and begins to wash the disciples' feet. A moment later he says to them, "If I, your Lord and Teacher, have washed your feet, you also ought to wash one another's feet. For I have set you an example, that you also should do as I have done to you" (John 13:14-15). So we Christians understand ourselves to be a *servant* people, following the example of our Teacher and Lord.

Robert Holland, a Presbyterian minister before he died, spent his summer vacations at the Chautauqua Institute in New York State. One summer he had a neighbor who was a sculptor. "I've been thinking of sculpting you a figure of Jesus," said the neighbor. "What do you think his most characteristic pose would be?" Holland thought long and hard about the question. What is the most characteristic pose of Jesus Christ? Is it the *teaching* Christ sitting on the slope of Mount Beatitude, the *healing* Christ reaching out to touch someone in need, the *crucified* Christ nailed to the cross of Calvary, or, maybe, the *resurrected* Christ standing in front of the empty tomb? Finally Holland replied, "I know what I'd like. I'd like you to carve me a statue of Christ with the towel washing the disciples' feet. That's the Christ I want the world to know — the *serving* Christ, the one who gives of himself for others."[1] "It *is* more blessed to give than to receive." Don't you agree?

Occasionally, however, we Christians discover that receiving is just as important as giving. Yet, for many of us, receiving is much more difficult. Consider, for example, Peter Gomes, the minister to Harvard University. Early in his career while teaching at Tuskegee Institute in Alabama, he received invitations to preach from the pulpits of small, rural, black Baptist churches in Macon County. These little churches paid the visiting preacher by taking up a "love offering" immediately following the sermon, which, according to Gomes, became "something of a referendum on preacher and sermon alike"! "Early on," he writes, "I refused these offerings on the grounds that these poor people and their poor church needed the money more than I did, since I had a decent salary from the institute, after all, and it was my pleasure to give." But when Gomes mentioned his refusals to the dean of women at Tuskegee, she thundered, "Who are you to refuse to accept the gift of these humble people? You have given insult by refusing to let them do what they can for you."[2] Sometimes, you see, it is more difficult to receive than to give.

Most every congregation has a handful of saints like the woman about whom I'm thinking: Active in church all her life, she was one of the most tireless and selfless members of the congregation. While many of the members drove late-model luxury cars, she zoomed around town in a nine-year-old Honda Civic. Her wardrobe was similarly out of date. But with a shrug of the shoulder she'd say, "I can think of more important things on which to spend my money." When a couple would arrive home from the hospital with a brand new baby, she'd be the first to drop by with a casserole, a plate of cookies, and a word of advice to the nervous parents about how to change a diaper or give the baby a bath. When the church needed someone to organize a potluck supper, fold the Sunday bulletins, or even tackle the troublesome junior high Sunday school class, she — God bless her! — would be the first to volunteer.

But then, tragically, she suffered a stroke, which left her partially paralyzed. Other church members tried to offer to help her, but she refused, fiercely independent soul that she was. "Thank you, dear," she would say, "but I can get by just fine by myself." Finally, in exasperation one of the deacons said, "She has been a care-giver all her life. But now she needs to learn how to receive help as well as give it." For her, and for many of us, it is more difficult to receive than to give.

So it was for Simon Peter, and, perhaps, for the other disciples as well. For when Jesus takes a towel and a basin of water, Peter protests. "Lord, are you going to wash my feet? You will never wash my feet" (John 13:6, 8). I have a book on my study shelf that is filled with famous paintings of biblical scenes. The book includes a thirteenth century work by an unknown French artist that shows Jesus washing Peter's feet while the other disciples watch and reluctantly wait their turn. The two disciples to Peter's left, knowing they are next in line, are nervously brushing the dirt from their *own* feet before Jesus gets to them.[3] How strange, but how characteristic of human nature!

If the truth be known, most of us don't like to receive help, especially not from our friends, not even when that friend is Jesus. We want to succeed in life on our own. We've been brought up to be self-sufficient, self-reliant, and to pull ourselves up by our own bootstraps. Like Peter we prefer to stand on our own two feet. "Lord, are you going to wash my feet?" he asks. "You will never wash my feet."

But Jesus replies, "Unless I wash you, you have no share with me" (John 13:8). Jesus, filled with divine wisdom, understood how hard it is to be a disciple. No matter how many positive thoughts we think; no matter how many kind words we speak; no matter how many good deeds we perform, the world will eventually wear us down unless the grace we receive is as great as the grace we try to give. As the dean of women put it to Peter Gomes, "You will never be able to give, until you learn how to be a generous receiver."[4]

Near the end of *The Longing For Home*, Frederick Buechner observes that Saint Paul begins virtually every one of his New Testament letters with words of grace. Says Buechner:

> *[Paul] points out that this grace he wishes them is "from God our Father and the Lord Jesus Christ" because he wants there to be absolutely no doubt about that. Grace is the best he can wish them because grace is the best he himself ever received.*[5]

No where is this grace of God and the Lord Jesus Christ more tangible than in the Upper Room on the night of Jesus' betrayal. For during supper, Jesus got up from the table and laid down his robe, which in the opinion of eminent New Testament scholar Raymond Brown is a symbol of the way Jesus will soon lay down his life on the cross,[6] and he began to wash the disciples' feet.

Like Peter, we continue to protest. "Lord, you will never wash our feet." Like Peter, we want to get by in life on our own. But Jesus reminds us that whatever power we possess for Christian living is not our own. It comes from him. "Unless I wash you, you have no share with me." "You will never be able to give," he seems to say, "until you learn how to be a generous receiver."

---

1. Robert Cleveland Holland, *Robert Holland At Shadyside* (Pittsburgh: published by Shadyside Presbyterian Church, 1985), pp. 22-23.

2. Peter J. Gomes, *The Good Book: Reading The Bible With Heart And Mind* (New York: William Morrow and Company, Inc., 1996), pp. 310-311.

3. Richard Muhlberger, ed., *The Bible In Art: The New Testament* (New York: Portland House, Publishers, 1990), pp. 110-111.

4. Gomes, p. 311.

5. Frederick Buechner, *The Longing For Home* (San Francisco: Harper Collins Publishers, Inc., 1996), p. 175.

6. Raymond E. Brown, *The Gospel According To John (xiii-xxi)* in the Anchor Bible Series, (Garden City, New York: Doubleday & Company, Inc., 1970), p. 551.

Good Friday
John 18:1—19:42

Looking At Life From The Point Of View Of Death

As part of my preparation for ministry, I participated in a program called Clinical Pastoral Education, or C.P.E. for short. The purpose of C.P.E. is to teach clergy to become more effective pastors: to make better hospital visits, to counsel people who are dying, to comfort those who are grieving. One day during class our instructor asked us to take out a piece of paper and a pen. Then he gave us these instructions:

> *During the next twenty minutes, I want each of you to write your own obituary. Imagine that you are going to die soon. How would you want to be remembered? Write an article about yourself for the obituary page of the newspaper.*

To say the least, it was a difficult assignment and not just because it forced us to come to terms with our own mortality. It was difficult because it asked us to look at life from the point of view of our own death. It was as if someone were asking, "What about your life is worth remembering from the perspective of death?" One woman in the class was overwhelmed by the assignment. She said, "I can't do it! How can I write, 'She had two homes and a boat'? That's all my life has been."

Each year Good Friday invites us to look at the life of Jesus from the point of view of his passion and death. According to the Gospel of John, the very last words Jesus spoke from the cross were the words, "It is finished" (John 19:30). What did he mean?

When we speak of something or someone as being finished, often we are speaking in terms of failure. For example, when Michael Jordan retired from professional basketball, people said of the Chicago Bulls, "They're finished." In other words, without Jordan the Bulls didn't stand a chance of winning another championship. When you embarrass your boss at an important meeting and afterwards he says to you, "You're finished," chances are good you are not about to get a promotion! When a student taking a final exam realizes that she forgot to study the correct material, she might say to herself, "I'm really finished now," and chances are she is not about to complete the exam in record time. Often when we speak of someone or something as being finished, we are speaking about failure, despair, defeat.

But when Jesus cries out from the cross, "It is finished," he is saying something different. He is not saying, "I'm all washed up, I'm no good, I'm a failure, I'm a flop." Rather, he is saying something like this, "I have lived the life that God intended me to live, a life of service and self-sacrifice that led me to this cross, and now, 'It is finished,' " which is to say — it is accomplished, it is completed, it is fulfilled. As such, Jesus' final words from the cross are not a pathetic and weary cry of defeat, but a triumphant and glorious shout of victory. "It is finished" — I have done with my life what I set out to do and I have glorified God by doing it.

As we thumb through John's Gospel we have the growing sense that Jesus' whole life is pointing toward his death on the cross. As early as the first chapter, John the Baptist sees Jesus approach and says of him, "Here is the Lamb of God (that is, the sacrificial lamb) who takes away the sin of the world!" (John 1:29). Not long after, at the wedding in Cana of Galilee, Jesus' mother lets him know that they have run out of wine. He replies, "What concern is that to you and to me. My hour has not yet come" (John 2:4). Twice more, John repeats those same words — "his hour had not yet come, his hour had not yet come" (John 7:30, 8:20) — until finally just prior to his betrayal and arrest, Jesus announces:

"The hour has come for the Son of Man to be glorified. Very truly, I tell you, unless a grain of wheat falls

> *into the earth and dies, it remains just a single grain; but if it dies, it bears much fruit."* — John 12:23-24

Some time later as Jesus looks down from the cross, his whole life flashes before his eyes. Then, with both courage and confidence he cries out, "It is finished — I have done with my life what I set out to do, and I have glorified God by doing it."

What do *you* see when you look at life from the point of view of your own death? When the time comes for you to breathe your last breath, will you be able to look back and say with Jesus, "It is finished — I have lived the life that God intended me to live"? Or will you look back regretfully on dreams that you never realized, broken relationships you were unable to fix, a purpose or meaning for your life which you never discovered? How important, therefore, to look at whatever time we have left from the point of view of our own death.

"It is finished," cried Jesus, and clearly there is a sense in which his words speak of finality and completion. But there is also a sense in which they speak not of an end but a great beginning. For didn't Jesus, himself, look beyond the agony of the cross to the glory of the resurrection? Didn't he say, "Destroy this temple, and in three days I will raise it up" (John 2:19)? Didn't he promise us his everlasting presence when in the Upper Room he said to his disciples:

> *"I will not leave you orphaned; I am coming to you. In a little while the world will no longer see me, but you will see me; because I live, you also will live. On that day you will know that I am in my Father, and you in me, and I in you."* — John 14:18-20

Did you notice what he said? "Because I live, you also will live." Most often we understand those words in terms of life after death, and well we should. Jesus himself said as much:

> *"In my Father's house there are many dwelling places. If it were not so, would I have told you that I go to prepare a place for you? And if I go and prepare a*

place for you, I will come again and will take you to myself, so that where I am, there you may be also."
— John 14:2-3

While his words speak about life in the hereafter, they also speak about life in the here and now. "Because I live," he says, "you also will live," *right here, right now, right in this very moment of time.*

How else can you explain why a man, who for most of his life turned his back on God, is now deeply involved in a local church, soaking up every bit of worship, education, fellowships and mission the church has to offer? What happened to him? Could it be that the redemptive work of Jesus Christ that began on the cross is not finished with him, but just beginning?

How else can you explain why a husband and wife continue to visit their former neighbor at the nursing home, even though he no longer recognizes them because of Alzheimer's Disease? Could it be that the redemptive work of Jesus Christ that began on the cross is not finished with them, but just beginning?

How else can you explain why so many people: hammer and nail for Habitat For Humanity, collect canned goods for the food pantry, give from glad and generous hearts, work for justice and peace in the world, and try to live moral lives that are pure and righteous before God? Could it be that the redemptive work of Jesus Christ that began on the cross is not finished with them, but just beginning?

Hanging on the cross, Jesus looked at his whole life from the point of view of his death. And what he saw pleased him, as it undoubtedly pleased God. No wonder he cried out with his dying breath, "It is finished!"

Easter
John 20:1-18

Resurrection In
A Cross-Shaped World

In one of his songs, Paul Simon of Simon and Garfunkel fame suggests that we live in a time "of miracle and wonder."[1] Yes, these *are* the days of miracle and wonder, and this is especially true of Easter. Can you think of any other day that contains more miracle and wonder than Easter? That's why we're here this morning, why the pews are especially crowded today, why we're decked out in our best Easter clothes, why we've covered the communion table with fragrant lilies, each of them like a miniature trumpet proclaiming the resurrection. That's why our choir is in tip-top form with beautiful brass accompaniment. That's why even those who rarely darken the door of the church the rest of the year are here today! Because this is a day of miracle and wonder, and we want to be part of it.

However, as someone has written, all of the wonderful things going on around us on Easter remind us "... that nothing even close to all that wonderful is going on inside of ourselves."[2] I think I know about that. A quick glance at the calendar says that it's Easter, but a review of my daily appointment book reads more like Good Friday. Rarely, will people sit down with the minister to talk about the joys of life. Rather, they come to talk about pain, suffering, and grief:

- a marriage which began with the promise "as long as we both shall live," has died an early death and led to a painful divorce;
- a faithful employee, loyal to the same company for years, has just been let go;

- a high school senior, a good student, is surprisingly wait-listed by the college of his choice;
- a middle-aged man estranged from his own parents says, "I just hope our next contact is not when one of them dies";
- a father is concerned about his troubled teenager;
- a wife is in anguish over her alcoholic husband.
- Some come and share their frustrations about the state of our nation: the wealth of the suburbs and the poverty of the inner city, the erosion of personal morality, the political posturing, and the scandals of Washington.
- And, of course, there are those who want to talk about death and grief: the first-time parents with the miscarriage, the dutiful son who watches helplessly as Alzheimer's makes mush of his father's brain; the lonely widow who still can't believe that her husband of 49 years is gone.

The calendar says Easter, but you'd never know it by the tears in our eyes.

"Mary stood weeping outside the tomb" (John 20:11), writes John, weeping, we presume, not only because they had crucified Jesus, not only because she is grieving his death, but weeping because someone has stolen his body. Or so she thinks. "They have taken away my Lord, and I do not know where they have laid him" (John 20:13).

John does not describe the extent of Mary's grief. But those of us who have lost a loved one know something of what she's feeling. We come around the corner of the house and expect to see our loved one sitting in her favorite chair, but the chair is empty. Habitually, we set a place for him at the dinner table and then foolishly remember that he is gone. We pick up the telephone and wish to God that the voice on the other end is hers, but, of course, it's not. Writing shortly after the death of her very best friend, American poet Edna St. Vincent Millay puts it like this:

> *But your voice —*
> *... For the beauty of that sound*
> *That in no new way at all*
> *Ever will be heard again.*[3]

How painful to think we will never hear the voice of that loved one again. And that's why what happens next makes Easter all the more a day of miracle and wonder. Suddenly, Mary comes face to face with the Risen Christ. Only, she doesn't recognize him. Presumably, something about his resurrected appearance is different. Something leads her to believe that he is the gardener. He doesn't look like anything or anyone she had expected to see.

Morgan Roberts is a retired Presbyterian minister who used to serve a church in Pittsburgh. For years that church has broadcast its Sunday services on the radio, which means that the preacher becomes familiar to many who have never set foot in the church. One Saturday morning Roberts was speaking at another church in Pittsburgh. Prior to the speech, a woman leaned over to a friend and said, "I've heard Morgan Roberts on the radio, but I've never met him." Then looking in the direction of the speaker's table, she said, "Which one is he?" When the friend pointed toward the one with thinning gray hair, wearing a dark gray preacher's suit and a regimental stripe red and black tie, the woman exclaimed, "Oh my! He doesn't look anything like he is supposed to look!" It was only when he began to speak that she recognized his familiar voice. Later Roberts would quip, "I was not at all surprised. No Welshman ever looks as good as his voice sounds!"[4]

Something like that happened to Mary on that first Easter morning. She fails to recognize the Risen Christ until he speaks her name, "Mary!" It was the hearing of his voice when he called her by name that transformed her Good Friday grief into the miracle and wonder of Easter.

But then, strangely, that familiar voice spoke a disturbing word. "Do not hold on to me," he says, "for I have not yet ascended to the Father" (John 20:17). Do not hold on to him? Why in the world not? Isn't that the very thing we *want* to do when we've been reunited with a loved one — to wrap our arms around him and hug him to ourself? What kind of callous and uncaring Christ is this who says, "Do not hold on to me"?

Barbara Brown Taylor, the eloquent Episcopal priest, points out that the scripture never says that Mary reached out and tried to hold Jesus. His comment, she writes, was a peculiar thing to say, unless ...

> *Unless it was what she called him — my Teacher — the old name she used to call him ... but that was his Friday name and here it was Sunday — an entirely new day in an entirely new life.*[5]

"Do not hold on to me," says the Risen Christ. It is as if he says: Don't think that you can go back and pick up where we left off before Good Friday, because you can't. Don't think that you can re-live the past, because you can't. Don't think you can go back, sit on that grassy hillside, and listen to me teach, for you can't; from now on, you will teach others in my name. And don't think that you can go back to that day when I fed the hungry multitude with five barley loaves and two fish, because you can't; from now on, you will feed the hungry in my name. Life is going to be different, he says, totally different, now that I have been raised from the dead. For I am no longer just that rabbi, that teacher from Nazareth. Now I am the Risen and Living Lord who calls you to let go of the past and follow me into an entirely new day in an entirely new life. "Do not hold on to me," he says, do not hold on to the past.

But we do, at least some of us do some of the time. In one of my former congregations, a woman had lost her husband the winter before I began my ministry in that church. When I first met her and she spoke extensively about her husband, I thought it was perfectly normal. She was recently widowed; I'd never met the man to whom she'd been happily married all those years; she simply wanted to tell me what he was like. But as the months became years and her conversations began to sound like a broken record — she was always talking about him and never about herself and what tomorrow might bring — I began to realize that this was not healthy. She was holding on to the past; she was lost in a wilderness of Good Friday grief. She desperately needed to let go of her pain and embrace the miracle and wonder of Easter, but she could not. And nothing I said to her could change her mind.

But, it doesn't have to be that way. Part of what Easter means is that this cross-shaped world in which we live does not have the final word. If the Risen Christ could transform the cross of Calvary, the Roman means of capital punishment, into a symbol of faith, hope, and love, which we even proudly wear as jewelry, just think what he can do for the cross-shaped struggles of your life and mine.

In his best-selling book *The Road Less Traveled*, Christian psychiatrist Scott Peck writes about a young man named Ted. When he came to see Dr. Peck, Ted had lost his enthusiasm for life. All his life he had suffered one bitter disappointment after another. His parents had punished him when he was a boy by taking away what he wanted the most. His brothers had teased him relentlessly. A young woman had dumped him the week before he went off to college. His best friend had been killed in a car accident during their sophomore year of college. When he was young, Ted had believed in God but gradually he began to shut God out, blaming God for all the bad things that had happened to him.

One day in one of his sessions with Dr. Peck, Ted recalled a time when he had nearly drowned. When Peck asked Ted how he felt about being saved, Ted said, "I guess I was fortunate."

"Fortunate?" asked the doctor. "Just an unusual coincidence?"

"I guess I was lucky," said Ted.

"Lucky?" asked Peck. "It's interesting, Ted, that when something painful happens to you, you rail against God. You rail against what a crappy, terrible world this is. But when something good happens, you guess you're lucky. A minor tragedy and it's God's fault. A miraculous blessing and you're a bit lucky."

To make a long story short, gradually Ted began to get well. With Dr. Peck's help and by the grace of God, he was able to let go of his painful past and reclaim his enthusiasm for life and for God. Then one day, Peck noticed something different about the check Ted made out to pay for his appointment. Instead of "Ted," he had signed his name *Theodore*. When Peck asked him about it, Ted told him that his aunt once urged him to be proud of the name Theodore because it means "lover of God." He said, "I was proud, but then my brothers made fun of me. 'Sissy choir boy,' they said, 'why don't you go kiss the altar.' So I became embarrassed by the name. But now I'm no longer embarrassed. I've decided to use my full name again. After all, I am a lover of God, aren't I?"[6]

Outside the tomb on Easter morning, the Risen Christ called Mary by name and invited her to let go of the past and follow him into a whole new day and a whole new life. He continues to call out to us today: "Theodore, Sally, Alice, Albert." Such, at least in part, is the miracle and the wonder of Easter.

---

1. Paul Simon, "The Boy in the Bubble" from the *Graceland* CD, Warner Brothers Records, 1986.

2. Frederick Buechner, *The Longing For Home* (San Francisco: Harper Collins Publishers, 1996), p. 144.

3. Edna St. Vincent Millay, "Elegy" in *Contemporary American Poetry*, H. Lincoln Foster, ed. (New York: Macmillan Company, 1963), pp. 36-37.

4. F. Morgan Roberts, *Are There Horses In Heaven?* (Pittsburgh: Lighthouse Point Press, 1996), p. 17.

5. Barbara Brown Taylor, "The Unnatural Truth" in *The Christian Century*, March 20-27, 1996, p. 325.

6. M. Scott Peck, *The Road Less Traveled* (New York: Simon and Schuster, Publishers, 1978), pp. 210-221.

Easter 2
John 20:19-31

Doubting Thomas
And His Twin

Several years ago the Episcopal Church launched a creative and clever advertising campaign. One of their ads pictured a young man with a frustrated look on his face because someone had put a heavy piece of tape across his mouth. His mouth had been taped shut; he was unable to speak. The caption, which accompanied the picture, said this: "The problem with churches that have all of the answers is that you can't ask questions."

Unfortunately, there *are* churches like that, churches which discourage dialogue, squelch questions, and disapprove of anyone who doubts. In one of his books, Lloyd Ogilvie, who is a Presbyterian minister and Chaplain of the United States Senate, recalls a conversation he had with a man named Mike. "I used to be a member of a church," confessed Mike, "but they said it was a sin to doubt — so I left." "Come to my church," Ogilvie said with a chuckle. "It's full of doubters!" Mike went on to say that his former pastor not only discouraged his doubts, but told him that it was a danger to doubt any aspect of the Christian faith and warned him that his doubts would become like a virus which would infect the whole church.[1]

I wonder whether Thomas — Doubting Thomas as we've come to call him — would be welcome in a church like the church Mike used to attend? Probably not. Any church that says that doubt is synonymous with sin would shun Thomas. How strange, then, that Thomas was welcomed as one of the twelve disciples. How ironic, that Jesus himself picked Thomas — doubts and all! — to be one of his closest followers.

As you may know, Thomas got the nickname *Doubting* Thomas because of a conversation that occurred shortly after the first Easter. The disciples have all gathered in a house in Jerusalem but Thomas is not with them. Suddenly, the Risen Christ appears to them, shows them the wounds in his hands and side, breathes new life into their deflated spirits and commissions them for the work of ministry. Later when Thomas returns, the other disciples can hardly wait to tell him the good news: "We have seen the Lord," they say. But Thomas replies, "Unless I see the mark of the nails in his hands, and put my finger in the mark of the nails and my hand in his side, I will not believe" (John 20:25). He doubted; he was unable to believe, and ever since we've been calling him Doubting Thomas.

While Thomas has his doubts, he is not the sinner that some people want to label him. In fact, according to theologian Douglas John Hall, "the line between faith and doubt is almost invisible."[2] Doubt is not the opposite of faith, as some would have us believe; rather, for many people doubt is an integral part of faith. Down through the years lots and lots of Christians have arrived at the land of faith by means of the back roads of doubt. Consider, for example, Christian writer C. S. Lewis as he is pictured in the popular movie *Shadowlands*. As a young man, Lewis fought as a British soldier in "the war to end all wars," which we've come to call World War I. During the war Lewis saw his best friend killed. He saw hundreds of other young men maimed and killed, "boys" who should have been attending university, rowing with the crew team, and "... lying on the emerald grass of Oxford's quads, with their heads on the soft laps of the dainty young girls whom they should in normal times be marrying." In utter agony, Lewis cried out to God for answers, "Why?" he asked with tears in his eyes. "If a good God made the world, why has it gone wrong?" Yet as Lewis matured, he came to realize that the more he questioned, the more his faith grew.[3]

Then there is Donald Coggan, who served as the 101st Archbishop of Canterbury. In one of his books he writes: "I am more of an agnostic today than when I was an undergraduate 45 years ago. That would make a good headline in the newspaper, wouldn't it?"

he quipped. "Agnostic Archbishop Sounds Off About Doubt."[4] What he means, of course, is this — that there are more areas of life over which he would put the sentence, "I don't know," than there were when he was a brash undergraduate. He goes on to add: "In what I believe are the essentials of the Christian faith, I should like to think I am a stronger and deeper believer."[5]

Or consider Annie Dillard. In her beautifully written memoir, *An American Childhood*, Dillard describes her teenage struggles with faith when she attended the Shadyside Presbyterian Church in Pittsburgh. Critical of the prim and proper piety of that Presbyterian Church, Dillard writes:

> *It was not surprising, really, that I alone in this church knew what the barefoot Christ, if ever there had been such a person, would think about things — grape juice, [elders in] tailcoats, [the minister's] British [accent], sable stoles ... After all, I was the intelligencia around these parts, single-handedly.*[6]

But as she looked down from the balcony, she noticed the whole congregation bowing their heads in prayer. Maybe they were *pretending* to pray, she quipped. But then, she grew critical of her own criticisms. She writes:

> *I began to doubt my own omniscience ... I was alert enough now to feel, despite myself, some faint, thin stream of spirit braiding forward from the pews ... The people had been praying ... to God, just as they seemed to be praying. That was the fact. I didn't know what to make of it.*[7]

Today, Annie Dillard is an active member of a Roman Catholic parish.

Do you know the name of Doris Betts? A Presbyterian elder, a Sunday school teacher, a part-time church organist, and for more than 25 years a member of the English Department at the University of North Carolina at Chapel Hill, Betts has written several short stories and four novels. In the summer of 1998 she received the Distinguished Writer Award at the Presbyterian Writers' Guild luncheon at the General Assembly which met in Charlotte. Yet, several years ago she spoke about her struggle with the Christian faith and described herself as a member of the "Tribe of Thomas."[8]

Scott Peck, the Christian psychiatrist, says that there is no such thing as a good hand-me-down religion. Writes Peck: "To be vital ... our religion must be a wholly personal one, forged entirely through the fire of our own questioning and doubting in the crucible of our own experience of reality."[9] So it was for Thomas, and so it is for many of us. John tells us that Thomas was called "the twin." Presumably, that means he was a twin and had a twin. Although we don't know anything about that biological twin, we can imagine that he's had many twins all across the years, *spiritual* twins, who tend to doubt, who find it hard to believe. Doubting Thomas had a twin; maybe that twin is someone like you, someone like me!

Those of us who call ourselves twins of Thomas might find hope in a couple of subtle details of the story. First, notice the day of the week that the Risen Christ appears to Thomas. John writes that it is "a week later" (John 20:26). A week after what? A quick review of the preceding verses suggests that one week earlier was Easter, and here it is now, the Sunday after Easter.

Could this be John's skillful way of reminding the reader of the importance of Christian worship — that in the midst of Sunday worship we become more aware of the presence of the risen Christ than we do the rest of the week. This is not to say that people cannot experience the Risen Christ at work or at play, around the conference table or while strolling down the seventh fairway. But it is to suggest that Sunday worship, more than at any other time, is the occasion when we are most likely to sense the Risen One in our midst. It just may be that nothing more glamorous than Sunday worship is the very place where those of us who doubt can discover a faith of our own and eventually exclaim with Thomas, "My Lord and my God" (John 20:28)!

Another interesting detail of the story is related to the first. John not only tells us that the Risen Christ appeared to Thomas on the Sunday after Easter, he also tells us that Christ appeared in the

midst of the *community*. Thomas was not alone; rather, he was among those who were gathered in Jesus' name (John 20:26). Have you even considered the many ways that the community of faith helps its individual members move from doubt to faith? Think about:
- the Sunday school teacher who encourages her students to fashion a faith they can call their own;
- the youth group leader who helps a thoughtful teenager reconcile the theory of evolution with the creation stories in Genesis;
- the sermon which allows the first-time visitor to reconnect with God after having spent years in a spiritual wilderness.
- Even the Affirmation of Faith, hardly the most dynamic part of worship, can help us work through our doubts.

In one of her books Barbara Brown Taylor writes about a friend who was struggling with the Creed. Taylor told her that it's important to think of the creed, not in the singular but the plural. When the whole congregation rises to confess what they believe, Taylor says:

> *I count on [others] to believe what I cannot believe ... right now. When my faith limps, I lean on the faith of the church, letting "our" faith suffice until "mine" returns ... My decision to say the creed at all is a decision to trust those who have gone before me.*[10]

There may be no better Sunday of the year to ponder the relationship between doubt and faith than the Sunday after Easter, when the lilies have begun to wither, the trumpets have been packed away until next year, and the over-flow crowds we experienced last week will not return until Christmas Eve. In the meantime, we have more than enough to sustain us. Not only do we have the presence and support of one another, we also have the belief that when two or three gather in the name of the Risen Christ, he will be with us.

1. Lloyd J. Ogilvie, *If God Cares, Why Do I Still Have Problems?* (Waco: Word Books, Publisher, 1985), pp. 210-211.

2. Douglas John Hall, *Thinking The Faith: Christian Theology In A North American Context* (Minneapolis: Fortress Press, 1991), p. 250.

3. Leonore Fleischer, *Shadowlands*, a novel based on the film by Richard Attenborough (New York: Signet Books, Publishers, 1993), pp. 8-9.

4. F. Donald Coggan, *Christ And Our Crises* (Waco: Word Books, Publisher, 1975), p. 20.

5. *Ibid.*

6. Annie Dillard, *An American Childhood* (New York: Harper & Row, Publishers, 1987), p. 197.

7. *Ibid.*, pp. 198-199.

8. W. Dale Brown, "The Big Questions: An Interview With Doris Betts" in *The Christian Century*, October 8, 1997, p. 870.

9. M. Scott Peck, *The Road Less Traveled* (New York: Simon and Schuster, Publishers, 1978), p. 194.

10. Barbara Brown Taylor, *The Preaching Life* (Cambridge: Cowley Publications, 1993), p. 71.

**Easter 3
Luke 24:13-35**

Wide-Eyed Recognition

With the miracle and wonder of Easter Day still a recent and very pleasant memory, we would do well to ponder Easter's enduring appeal. In an article in *The Washington Post*, Bill Broadway offered this description of Easter:

> *Churches are festooned with bright flowers celebrating the Resurrection of Jesus, huge choirs sing of the joy of renewal, and worshippers crowd into tiny churches or gigantic cathedrals. Attendance swells to a level unimaginable at any other time of year, including Christmas.*[1]

Broadway hit that nail on the head! Most churches attract twice as many worshipers for Easter services as they do on a typical Sunday. Packed into the pews on Easter, and often rubbing elbows with one another, are the faithful and the curious, the believers and the skeptics, the spiritually sensitive and those with hearts of stone. As hard as it is to imagine, surveys suggest that more than half of our nation's adults and their children — at least 120 million people — attend worship on Easter Day![2]

Why do they all come on Easter; and why do so few of them return on the Sundays that follow? Undoubtedly, some come because of custom or convention. These days attending church is no longer as fashionable as it once was; but attending church *on Easter* still ranks near the top of the rites of spring. Others come because they're in town for the weekend visiting family or friends, still others to appease a spouse or set a good example for a child. Perhaps a few even come because they need something to do before Sunday brunch! Ralph Sockman, the great Methodist minister of a generation or so ago, once joked that some of his parishioners thought so highly of his preaching that they pledged to the church 500 dollars or even 1,000 dollars just to hear one of his sermons. Then he added, "Of course, they hear only *one* sermon per year — on Easter!"

To be fair about it, though, most people come to church on Easter because they have heard this outlandish claim about Jesus rising from the dead, and they want to know whether or not it is true. So they come, believers and skeptics alike, hoping to be inspired by the beautiful music, hoping to catch the enthusiasm of the huge crowd of people, hoping that the preacher will give them some proof that Christ is not dead but alive. "Is he really alive?" we all wonder, "and if so, how can we recognize his presence in our midst and in our world?"

In one of its memorable scriptures, the Church offers a simple, straightforward answer to these questions. Chapter 24 of Luke tells us about two of Jesus' disciples walking along the road to Emmaus. It is the afternoon of the first Easter, and like us, these two disciples had heard a claim about Jesus rising from the dead. "Could it be true?" they wonder as they walk along the way. "Is it possible that Jesus is not dead but alive? But he was crucified," they say arguing with their own sensibilities, "crucified, dead and buried. When you're dead, you're dead. This rumor of resurrection can't be true, can it? Is it anything more than 'an idle tale'?" (Luke 24:11).

While they were talking about these things, the Risen Christ came near and went with them but, says Luke, "their eyes were kept from recognizing him" (Luke 24:16). *Something* kept them from recognizing him, but what could that something be? Maybe that something had to do with Christ himself. Maybe something about his appearance kept them from recognizing him. After all, this is not the only time when the disciples fail to recognize the Risen Christ.

- When the Risen Christ appears to Mary outside the garden tomb, she fails to recognize him — she mistakes him for the gardener — until he calls her by name (John 20:14-16).
- When the disciples are out in the boat fishing all night long with not a single fish to show for their efforts, the Risen Christ stands on the beach and calls out to them, "but," says John, "the disciples did not know that it was Jesus" (John 21:4).

Maybe that something that kept the disciples from recognizing the Risen Christ had to do with Christ himself — his resurrected appearance, demeanor, countenance.

On the other hand, maybe that something that kept them from recognizing him had more to do with *them* than with him. In an essay in *The Christian Century*, Presbyterian minister Susan R. Andrews suggests:

> *Modern disciples come straggling through the church door weighed down by cynicism, stress, pretense, power ... They, like the first disciples, yearn for the living presence of God. But they are too preoccupied, too suspicious, too busy to actually recognize God. In their objective world of fact and truth and matter and money, the church's world of mystery and meaning and risk and relationship seems silly.*[3]

Whatever it was, *something* kept them from recognizing him. And so they speak to him — this incognito Christ — as if he were a stranger. They recite to him their litany of lament. They tell him about:

> *"Jesus of Nazareth, who was a prophet mighty in deed and word before God and all the people, and how our chief priests and leaders handed him over to be condemned to death and crucified him. But we had hoped that he was the one to redeem Israel. Yes, and besides all this, it is now the third day since these things took place. Moreover, some women of our group astounded*

> *us. They were at the tomb early this morning, and when they did not find his body there, they came back and told us that they had indeed seen a vision of angels who said that he was alive. Some of those who were with us went to the tomb and found it just as the women had said; but they did not see him."*
>
> — Luke 24:19-24

After the two disciples recite their litany, Jesus interprets the scriptures for them. Later, when they arrive at their destination, Jesus appears to be going further, but they invite him into the house to have something to eat. As they sit down at the table, suddenly the guest becomes the host and Jesus takes the bread, blesses it, breaks it, and gives it to them. At that moment, a moment of wide-eyed wonder, they recognize him in the breaking of the bread. Then, they get up and return to Jerusalem to tell the other disciples about their experience with the Risen Christ.

The reason the early Church remembered this story and preserved it in its scriptures is because it bears a remarkable resemblance to what we Christians do on every Sunday of the church year — namely, gather in a place like this to worship. Don't miss the parallels between this resurrection story and Sunday worship! Notice how the events unfold. These two Christians are walking along the way. Incidentally, the early Christians often spoke of themselves as "people of the way," and here are these two walking along "the way" or the road. As they walk along, the Risen Christ comes into their midst. They summarize the gospel for him. He, in turn, interprets the gospel for them. Then they sit at table and break bread. And in the midst of that — call to worship, scripture, sermon, communion — in the midst of something as dull and drab as Sunday worship, their eyes are opened and they recognize the Risen Christ in their midst. No wonder they get up from the table and go out to tell others about their experience.

Of course, most of us want something more than an *experience* of the Risen Christ. We want some mighty and majestic proof positive that Christ has been raised from the dead. We want objective truth. But most preachers realize that we have none to offer. Do you know, for example, that the Risen Christ never appears in the New Testament to anyone other than his friends and followers? Don't you wonder what might have happened had he appeared to Pontius Pilate, to Pilate's wife who had the dream about Jesus, or maybe even to Caiphas, the Jewish high priest? Don't you wonder how different things would have been had the Risen Christ appeared to people like that? But the New Testament doesn't indulge us with such fantasy. Instead, we hear one story after another about how Christ appeared to his friends, to those who had taken the time to know him, learn from him, love him, and serve him.

Perhaps this message comes as a disappointment to some of you. Undoubtedly, it would disappoint many of the curious who throng to church each year on Easter. What they want — and what many of us want as well — is proof, proof positive that Christ has been raised from the dead. Strangely, this sacred story offers no such proof. Rather, it gives us a glimpse of the simple conviction that sincere believers have had from the very beginning. When Christians gather to talk about the scriptures, hear them interpreted, and break bread with one another, miracle of miracles, our eyes are opened and we recognize the Risen Christ in their midst.

Christ is risen! We know that to be true, and we should proclaim it with every breath we possess even if we can't prove it. But, it's true, nevertheless, because we have experienced his living presence, not primarily on the golf course, or in some backyard garden, or at the beach, or when beholding a beautiful sunset. Rather, we have experienced his presence in the midst of other Christians who are doing nothing more spectacular than talking about the scriptures, hearing them interpreted, breaking bread and sharing the cup with one another, and then going out into the world to tell others about our experience. Then, like the two disciples on the road to Emmaus, we too will be able to say that Christ has been made known to us in the breaking of the bread.

---

1. Bill Broadway, "The Easter Turnout" in *The Washington Post*, April 3, 1999, p. B7.

2. *Ibid.*

3. Susan R. Andrews, "Holy Heartburn" in *The Christian Century*, April 7, 1999, p. 385.

**Easter 4
John 10:1-10**

Listening For The Voice
Of The Good Shepherd

I know a woman who says that her husband has a listening problem. Incidentally, this is not autobiographical. To be sure, he does have a hearing problem and wears hearing aids to compensate, but his real problem — at least according to his wife — is not a hearing problem but a listening problem. She says to him, "I'm going to the store, so would you please turn the oven to 350 degrees at 5:30 and put in the casserole." "Sure," he replies, "no problem." But when she comes home, the dinner is still cold. By the way, did I remember to tell you that this is not autobiographical! She says to him, "Would you please keep Saturday morning free. I need you to take the kids to the orthodontist." "Of course, honey," he answers. But when Saturday comes he suddenly remembers that he has something else to do — a conflict. "I can't take the kids to the orthodontist," he protests. "Why didn't you ask me sooner?"

Why do you suppose that husband has so much trouble listening to his wife? We might be tempted to explain it away by saying that he's just becoming forgetful. He's having one of those, so called "senior moments." Or maybe we could blame it on the male chromosome. Men are *born* not to listen to the important women in their lives, just as they are born not to ask for directions when they get lost! But such explanations seem too silly and simplistic for these complex times in which we live.

A better explanation would be to say this — we live in a time in which many different voices compete for our attention. And with so many voices crying out to us, it's hard to pay attention to the voices that really matter. Have you ever stopped to think about all of these competing voices? For example:

- There is the voice of success or career ambition, which says, "You want to be somebody, don't you? Don't you want to make a name for yourself? Don't you want to climb your way up the career ladder? Work harder" says this voice. "Become a success." And competing with this voice is the voice which says, "If you spend all your time striving for success, you won't have any time left for your boyfriend or your girlfriend, your beloved, your family. If you work 60 or 65 hours a week, how will you ever spend time with those who are most important to you?"
- There is the voice of consumerism, which tells you why you need this new car, this new computer, this new kitchen appliance, this new golf club, this new pair of shoes. "Go ahead," says the voice of consumerism, "spend, buy, accumulate — you deserve it; you are entitled to it." This is the voice that urges us to paste a bumper sticker on the back of the mobile home that says, "We're spending our grandchildren's inheritance." This is the voice that takes as its motto, "Shop Till You Drop." As Sharon Daloz Parks has written:

> Once, we only went to market. Now the market comes to us ... through television, telemarketing, magazines, catalogues, and online services. We wear advertising on our clothing and plaster it on every façade of our common life. And it works. Americans now spend more time and money shopping than do citizens of any other nation.[1]

And competing with this voice is the voice of simplicity, the voice that says, "Do you really need all of these things? Does filling your life (not to mention your house and your closet) with all this stuff make you a better person? Does it increase your self worth?" Why not try to live a simpler life, free from what the Quakers call "cumber"?

- There is the voice of community, which invites you to be part of something bigger than yourself. It is the voice that President Kennedy invoked in his Inaugural Address when he said, "Ask not what your country can do for you — ask what you can do for your country."[2] It is the voice that says, "Get involved. Give of your time and talent. Make a difference in our common life." And competing with this voice is the voice that says, "You need to look out for yourself. No one else is going to take care of you, so take care of yourself. Don't waste your time in the community. It's like putting a Band-Aid on a cancerous tumor. Instead, protect your own best interests. Collect, hoard, stockpile. If you don't look out for yourself, no one else will."
- There is the voice of faith, which invites you into a world of mystery and meaning and says to you, "Trust, believe, pray, have faith in things unseen." And competing with this voice is the voice of reason and common sense, which says to you, "You don't believe any of that religious nonsense, do you? Proof is what you need. Science is the answer to all your questions. Faith is for the birds!"

These are but a few of the many voices that compete daily for our attention. Is it any wonder why we find it so hard to pay attention to the voices that really matter? Is it any wonder why so many of us have a listening problem?

How fortunate, therefore, that into a world of many voices comes the one we call Jesus. In fact, his voice was so clear and compelling — indeed, his whole life was such a miracle of speech — that some of his followers began to refer to him as the *logos*, that is the Word of God in human form. "In the beginning was the Word," writes John in the prologue to his Gospel, "and the Word was with God and the Word was God" (John 1:1).

The tenth chapter of John offers us one of the most beautiful images found anywhere in the Bible. At the same time it makes one of the most radical claims in scripture. By association, it invites us to recall some of the most endearing words ever written, the words of Psalm 23:

The LORD is my shepherd; I shall not want. He maketh me to lie down in green pastures: he leadeth me beside the still waters. He restoreth my soul: he leadeth me in the paths of righteousness for his name's sake. Yea, though I walk through the valley of the shadow of death, I will fear no evil: for thou art with me; thy rod and thy staff they comfort me. Thou preparest a table before me in the presence of mine enemies: thou anointest my head with oil; my cup runneth over. Surely goodness and mercy shall follow me all the days of my life: and I will dwell in the house of the LORD for ever.

— Psalm 23 (KJV)

After leading us back to those green pastures beside the still waters, John says in essence, "If you really want to know what God is like, then look at Jesus. If you want to come face to face with that divine Shepherd about whom the psalmist wrote, then follow Jesus for he is the Good Shepherd." Not only that, says John, but this Good Shepherd "calls his own sheep by name ... and the sheep follow him because they know his voice" (John 10:3-4).

Some might think of the idea of the sheep knowing the voice of the shepherd is a romantic notion far removed from reality. But it's actually true. Those who travel to the Holy Land often return with stories of nomadic shepherds leading their flocks to "the still waters" of some gentle stream running through the desert. Three or four shepherds and several dozen sheep all crowd together at the same place. Then, when the time to leave comes, one by one the shepherds break off from the others and call out to their own sheep with a distinct whistle, a familiar word, or the shrill sound from a pipe. Amazingly, only some of the sheep follow because they know their shepherd's voice. They know to whom they belong.

Do you know to whom you belong? Do you realize that the words *longing* and *belonging* come from the same root word?[3] In other words, there is in each of us a longing to belong, a basic need to be part of something or someone to whom we can give our heart and soul. That is why some people join a club, a fraternity or a sorority; why others get lured into a gang or a cult. All of us long to belong to something or to someone.

- "Our souls are restless until they find their rest in thee," said Saint Augustine in a familiar quote.
- "It is not good that the man should be alone," said God at the time of creation. "I will make him a helper as his partner" (Genesis 2:18).
- "What is your only comfort in life and death?" asks the first question of The Heidelberg Catechism. Answer: "That I belong — body and soul, in life and death — not to myself but to my faithful Savior, Jesus Christ, who at the cost of his own blood has fully paid for all my sins."[4]

"I am the Good Shepherd," says Jesus. "The Good Shepherd lays down his life for the sheep" (John 10:11).

Have you noticed what this passage requires of us if we want to belong to the flock of the Good Shepherd? Nothing! We belong, not because of any effort or belief on our part; rather, we belong simply because the Good Shepherd claims us as his own. Sadly, some people assume that they can't belong if they are unable first to say what they believe. For them, believing precedes belonging. Such people need to hear the advice of Episcopal priest Barbara Brown Taylor. In one of her books she writes:

> *Please stop exiling yourself from the flock because of your beliefs about what it takes to belong ... we belong to the flock not because we are certain of God, but because God is certain of us ... whether you are here because you believe or because you want to believe, you are here because you belong to God's sheep.*[5]

Often we think that believing precedes belonging. However, in both life and faith the opposite is true most of the time. Belonging precedes believing. For example, when a first-grader places her hand above her heart and recites the words of the Pledge of Allegiance, does she understand all that it means to be an American? Of course not. But by reciting the words of the Pledge, she is affirming that she belongs, even if she is too young to express exactly what she believes.

It's the same for people of faith. When we decide to be part of the flock of the Good Shepherd, when we decide to belong, gradually we grow in our beliefs. Gradually we learn what it means to confess Christ as Savior and Lord. Gradually we realize that his voice is the one voice that really matters.

We live in a time in which many different voices compete for our attention. With so many voices crying out to us, how important to learn to listen to the voice of the Good Shepherd. The Good Shepherd "calls his own sheep by name and leads them out ... and the sheep follow him" — why? — "because they know his voice."

---

1. Sharon Daloz Parks, "Household Economics," *Practicing Our Faith*, Dorothy C. Bass, ed. (San Francisco: Jossey-Bass Publishers, 1997), pp. 45-46.

2. John F. Kennedy "Inaugural Address," *Great American Speeches*, Gregory R. Suriano, ed. (New York; Gramercy Books, 1993), pp. 219-220.

3. This insight is offered by Frederick Buechner, *The Longing For Home* (San Francisco: Harper Collins Publishers, 1996), p. 18.

4. The Heidelberg Catechism, in *The Book Of Confessions* (Louisville: Published by The Office of the General Assembly of the Presbyterian Church, 1994), 4.001.

5. Barbara Brown Taylor, *The Preaching Life* (Cambridge: Cowley Publications, 1993), pp. 144-145.

Easter 5
John 14:1-14

The Truth About Jesus

Believe it or not, there is a theological debate raging in our society at present in the strangest of all places. This debate is not taking place in some ivy-covered institution of theological learning; nor is it a subject for television commentators like Ted Koppel or Larry King. No, the debate is occurring — of all places — on the back of people's cars! It all began some years ago when people began to put a small fish symbol on the back of their cars. For those of you who don't know about such things, since the early days of Christianity the fish has been a secret symbol among Christians. Those early Christians were living in a time of great persecution at the hands of the Romans and they needed some secret symbol that would identify them to one another but not to those who would do them harm. The fish symbol served that purpose perfectly, because the spelling of the Greek word for fish, *ichthus*, also formed an anagram which means "Jesus Christ, God's Son, Savior." Every time those early Christians saw the symbol of a fish, they remembered to think: "Jesus Christ, God's Son, Savior."

In recent years, a number of Christians have begun to put the fish symbol on the back of their cars. Nothing very controversial about that, hardly the basis for a heated debate, at least initially. But what began to happen was this. Some Christians began to display fish symbols, not with the word, *ichthus* — the Greek word for fish — inside, but with the word "truth" instead. Often, these were the same Christians who appeared before the local school board insisting that creationism be taught in the schools, side by side with the theory of evolution. And suddenly the bumper sticker debate swung into high gear. That initial non-controversial fish spawned an entire school of fish! One of them features a similar-looking fish, but this fish has little feet and inside the fish is the word, "Darwin." Still another fish has a little dome over its head and inside this fish is the word, "Alien." That, it seems, is somebody's humorous idea of how human beings first came to earth. Even our Jewish brothers and sisters have gotten into the act and in a wonderfully funny way at that. They have a fish bumper sticker of their own, and the word inside their fish is *Gefilte*, as in *gefilte fish*!

But the bumper sticker that takes the debate to a new level is the one which features two fish, a big fish with the word "Truth" on it and a small fish with the word "Darwin" on it, and the big fish is devouring the small fish. In other words, truth — at least the way some Christians define truth — is devouring science. In the great battle of the bumper stickers being waged on the highways and byways of our nation, biblical truth goes head to head with scientific truth, and in the end one of these claims to truth will devour the other. But does it have to come to that?

If I were in the bumper sticker business, I would design a bumper sticker that also features two fish. I would make them both the same size. One would feature the word, *ichthus*, the anagram that means "Jesus Christ, God's Son, Savior," and the other would feature the word, "Darwin." And I would have these two fish facing each other and maybe even kissing each other. I hope these kissing fish would suggest that the truth claims of the Bible and the truth claims of science need not be mutually exclusive. Rather, they can exist side by side because the truths they proclaim are not contradictory but complementary.

While there are lots of Christians — primarily fundamentalist Christians — who argue that the Bible is historically and scientifically accurate to every last detail, there are many other Christians including most mainline Protestants who believe that the Bible is not a scientific text at all. For example, Walter Brueggemann, a professor at a Presbyterian seminary, has written:

> *Creation, as understood in the Bible, seeks to explain nothing. Creation faith is rather a doxological response, a hymn of praise, to the wonder that I, that we, that the world exist.*[1]

And Joseph Sittler, for years professor of theology at the University of Chicago, was both utterly serious and wonderfully whimsical when he wrote:

> *In the creation story we are told who we are. We are given our identity, and if we could understand that, we would stop worrying about whether the antelopes or the cantaloupes came in a certain order.*[2]

How then should we understand the truth claims of the Bible? Doesn't Pontius Pilate speak for many of us when he asks, "What is truth?" How should we reply?

In one of his books, Canadian theologian Douglas John Hall offers this helpful distinction. He says that the essence of our Christian belief is not that the words of the Bible are true in and of themselves. Rather, what is true is that to which the Bible points.[3] In its own way the Gospel of John draws the same distinction. Do you know, by the way, that the Gospel of John has more to say about "truth" than any other book in the New Testament?

On the one hand, the sixteenth chapter of the Gospel of John affirms that the "Holy Spirit will guide us into all truth" (see John 16:13). Notice that the text does not say that we have all of the truth already. Nor does the text claim to be the truth itself. Rather, the text affirms that the Spirit will *lead us* or *guide us* into the truth.

Certainly, we have seen this principle at work in the world of science. For centuries we humans believed that the earth rather than the sun was at the center of the universe. But in the sixteenth century, a Polish astronomer named Nicholas Copernicus said the opposite — the sun not the earth is at the center of the universe. Less than one hundred years later the Italian scientist and inventor Galileo supported the Copernican view of the universe, a position that earned him the wrath of the Roman Catholic Church. Although

Galileo considered himself a loyal Catholic, the Church did not. They tried him, found him guilty of heresy, and confined him to house arrest. Interestingly, the Church took some 350 years to repent of its mistake and restore Galileo to his position as one of the pioneers of modern science. Can you see what happened? For years the Church had clung to a truth claim that turned out to be a false claim, and ultimately the Spirit led Galileo and later the Church into the truth.

We see much the same thing in the life of faith. On more than one occasion, we Christians have changed our minds as the Spirit has led us to discover some deeper dimension of the truth. Consider, for example, the issue of slavery. For hundreds of years many Christians believed that slavery was a God-given and biblically justified right. But we've changed our minds about that as the Spirit has guided us into the truth. For hundreds of years we Christians believed that women should have no leadership role in the church. But some Christian denominations have changed our minds about that as the Spirit has led us into the truth, and as a result we have ordained women as pastors and other church leaders. For hundreds of years we believed that clergy should not marry people who had been divorced. But some years back a number of denominations, including the Presbyterian Church, began to allow their clergy to remarry divorced people. Why the change of belief? While we still want to honor the sanctity of marriage, while we still want to say that God's best hope is for a man and woman to live together as husband and wife till death do them part, we also want to say that sometimes we humans make mistakes. Sometimes we fall short of the life that God intends us to live. And when we do, we want to affirm the redemptive grace of God that gives us all, including divorced persons, the chance to start again. Can you see what happened? The Spirit has led us to affirm a new truth claim about the unmerited amazing grace of God.

All of this is by way of saying that the Bible continues to point us toward the truth that is still out ahead of us in the future. That truth is bigger, more complex, and more mysterious than any book — yes, even the Bible — can contain. There are some Christians who worship the Bible. We Presbyterians and most mainline Protestants do not. Rather, we worship the One to whom the Bible points. And that leads us to the other claim that the Gospel of John makes about the truth.

The fourteenth chapter of John records a conversation between Jesus and his disciples in which Jesus says that he *is* the truth. He does not say that he points to the truth, although his life may be the most truthful life ever lived; nor that his teachings sound like the truth, although many of them do; nor even that he is the way to the truth. Rather, the scripture makes the incredible, outlandish claim that Jesus himself is the truth. Do you remember the setting for this claim? Jesus is preparing the disciples for his departure. Soon he will go to the cross. He tells them that he is going to prepare a place for them in one of the rooms of God's heavenly realm. He assumes that they know the way. But Thomas replies, "Lord, we do not know where you are going. How can we know the way?" Jesus says to him, "I am the way, and the truth, and the life. No one comes to the Father except through me" (John 14:5-6).

What are we to do with this claim, particularly in these pluralistic times in which we live? After all, many of the people we encounter in daily life don't identify God with Jesus as we do, but with the Buddha, or Mohammed, or someone else. Can we continue to believe that Jesus is the truth, especially in a world of many, legitimate worldwide religions?

As we saw with the debate about the fish bumper stickers, people tend to take sides and to fall into one category or the other. On one side of the debate will be those who insist that Jesus is the truth and that he is the one and only way to God. They will point to the words of the text which say, "No one comes to the Father except through me," and they will insist that all other religious truth claims are false claims. Follow Jesus, they say, or risk eternal damnation because he is the only way to God. In the past, such a triumphant, exclusive approach launched the Crusades, burned heretics at the stake, and oppressed religious minorities, none of which seems consistent with the Jesus the New Testament proclaims as the truth.

The other side of the debate insists that Jesus was but one prophet among many, that ultimately all religions lead down the same path, that in the name of tolerance and inclusivity, we must never insist that Jesus is the truth. But as Douglas John Hall asks, are these the only two choices available to us: "... either to extol Jesus by excluding everybody who doesn't name that name, or to minimize his place in Christian faith in order to appear more accepting and inclusive?"[4]

Today many people are declaring that North America has become a mission field. Therefore, we might want to listen to the wisdom of those who have served as missionaries. Lesslie Newbigin was a minister of the United Reformed Church of the United Kingdom and spent years as a missionary in South India. This is what he has to say about Jesus and the truth:

> *The Church proclaims that Jesus is Lord. He is Lord not only of the Church but of the world, not only in the religious life but in all life, not merely over some people but over all peoples ... [And yet], we do not yet know all that it means to say that Jesus is Lord. We will have to learn as we go along ... We are missionaries, but we are also learners. We do not have all the truth, but we know the way along which truth is to be sought and found.*[5]

What is the truth about Jesus? For Christians like you and me, it is that Jesus himself is the truth.

---

1. Walter Brueggemann, *Texts Under Negotiation: The Bible And Postmodern Imagination* (Minneapolis: Fortress Press, 1993), p. 29.

2. Joseph Sittler, *Gravity And Grace* (Minneapolis: Augsburg Press, 1986), p. 36.

3. See Douglas John Hall, *Thinking The Faith: Christian Theology In A North American Context* (Minneapolis: Fortress Press, 1991), p. 120.

4. Douglas John Hall, *Why Christian? For Those On The Edges Of Faith* (Minneapolis: Fortress Press, 1998), p. 32.

5. Lesslie Newbigin, *Truth To Tell: The Gospel As Public Truth* (Grand Rapids: Eerdmans Publishing Company, 1991), p. 34.

Easter 6
John 14:15-21

Living In Two Worlds At Once

Here are two statements about the world. Tell me if both of them ring true for you. The first of them is this: "The world is a beautiful place." And the second statement is this: "The world is a terrible and dangerous place." Both statements are true — don't you agree? — and yet, ironically, they seem to say the exact opposite thing. How much easier it would be to affirm one statement or the other, but not both.

The world is a beautiful place — most of us can say that with no difficulty at all. The miracle of the birth of a baby, the splendor of a spectacular sunset, the wonder of music and poetry and art and drama — all of these affirm the beauty of the world in which we live. Joseph Sittler taught theology at the University of Chicago for years. Late in his life he began to go blind. His friends said to him, "Joe, if you had your full sight back for just one afternoon, what would you go and see?" Without any hesitation at all he said, "Chartres, the glories of the blues in the cathedral windows there are so beautiful."[1]

If you have ever beheld the beauty of the trees when they are aflame in their fall foliage, then you can identify with American poet Edna St. Vincent Millay when she wrote:

> *Thy woods, this autumn day, that ache and sag*
> *And all but cry with color!*
> *... Lord, I do fear*
> *Thou'st made the world too beautiful this year.*[2]

If you have ever looked into the nighttime sky at the moon and the planets and the shimmering stars which hang down like lovely lanterns in God's cosmic cathedral, then you know firsthand that the world is a beautiful place. Speaking of the cosmos, I know that every woman here believes that the world is a beautiful place. Do you know why? Because the word *cosmos*, the Greek word for "world," is the same word from which we get our word "cosmetics"! Ponder that the next time that you are applying your makeup. Yes, if there is one thing we can all affirm, it is that the world — the cosmos — is a beautiful place.

But the world is not only a beautiful place; it is also a terrible and dangerous place: every earthquake, tornado, or hurricane; every plane crash, like the tragic crash which took the life of young John Kennedy, his wife, and his wife's sister; every dreaded disease like cancer and AIDS; every random act of violence; every school ground shooting; every awful episode of ethnic cleansing; and every war which is ever fought — all of these events remind us that the world is a terrible and a dangerous place.

If only we could choose one or the other, we'd know how to live. If the world is beautiful, then we could embrace it. But if the world is terrible and dangerous, then we'd be better off to fear it and guard ourselves against it.

Like us, the Gospel of John struggles to make sense of the world. On the one hand John affirms that the world is good and worthy of God's love. After all, way back at the time of creation, God pronounced the world "good." And in the fullness of time, "God so loved the world that he gave his only Son, so that everyone who believes in him may not perish but may have eternal life. Indeed," continues John, "God did not send the Son into the world to condemn the world, but in order that the world might be saved through him" (John 3:16-17). The world, John wants us to know, is deeply loved by God.

But the world is also a dangerous place. For one thing, the world is a dark place, which needs the light of Christ to shine in it. "The light shines in the darkness," wrote John, "and the darkness did not overcome it" (John 1:5). For another thing, the world has rejected Christ. "He was in the world, and the world came into being through him; yet the world did not know him" (John 1:10). Can you see John's struggle to make sense of the world? The world in not just a beautiful place deeply loved by God, it is also a "godless world"[3] which has turned its back on Christ.

You might say, therefore, that John had a lover's quarrel with the world. Robert Frost, the American poet, once said that about himself. One day Frost was walking through a cemetery looking at the tombstones. He grew interested in the words inscribed on each tombstone, which attempted to sum up the person's life. Frost found himself asking, "What epitaph would I choose for my own tombstone?" These are the words engraved on his gravestone: "I had a lover's quarrel with the world."[4]

And so it was for the author of the Gospel of John. He too had a lover's quarrel with the world. He knew that the early Christians should be engaged in the world through mission because, after all, this is God's world, the world God loves, the world God sent Christ to save. But John also feared the corrupting influence of the world. He must have wondered as many have wondered since — how can we Christians be *in* the world without being *of* the world? How can we live in the world without being swallowed up by the world? How can we live in two different worlds at once?

Of course, the early Christians were not the first ever to face such a problem. Hundreds of years before, the people of ancient Israel faced a similar struggle during what we've come to call the Babylonian Captivity or the Babylonian Exile. They had been dragged away from their homeland and forced to live as prisoners of war in far-away Babylon. A beautiful poem from the Book of Psalms recalls their ordeal:

> *By the rivers of Babylon — there we sat down and there we wept when we remembered Zion. On the willows there we hung up our harps. For there our captors asked us for songs, and our tormentors asked for mirth, saying, "Sing us one of the songs of Zion!"*
> — Psalm 137:1-3

"Sing us one of the songs of your homeland," said the captors. And do you know how they answered? "How can we sing the Lord's song in a foreign land?" Indeed, how can *anybody* sing the Lord's song in a strange land? How can we live in this strange and secular world and at the same time hold on to what is spiritual and sacred?

Jesus knew that his disciples would face this very struggle in the world. So he gathered them in the Upper Room to prepare them. He knew that his time with them was winding down. Soon he would go to the cross. Soon he would be put to death. Soon he would leave them all alone, alone in a world that was both terrible and dangerous, a world that would swallow them alive unless they could define themselves in terms that were distinct from the world. So there in the Upper Room he spoke to them tenderly as if they were little children. There in the Upper Room he put before them both a challenge and a promise. The challenge was, at the same time, both simple and demanding. He stated the whole thing in just nine words: "If you love me," he said, "you will keep my commandments" (John 14:15).

Of course, not everybody likes the idea of commandments, of rules and regulations. "Did God really say that we can eat of the fruit of any tree in the garden, but not of *that* fruit?" But that temptation was too great for our spiritual ancestors Adam and Eve, and they did what they should not have done. Ever since, we humans have struggled to decide — should we live by the commandments that God has set before us, or should we do our own thing and hope that no one is watching?

Yet, as we mature most of us begin to realize that the commandments are not just rigid rules to obey. They are also good and gracious gifts of God to order and regulate our lives and which help to shape our identity and define who we are and how we might live. Once, someone said to Jesus, "Teacher, which commandment in the law is the greatest?" He answered, " 'You shall love the Lord your God with all your heart, and with all your soul, and with all your mind.' This is the greatest and first commandment. And a second is like it: 'You shall love your neighbor as yourself' " (Matthew 22:36-39). On another occasion Jesus said to his disciples, "I give you a new commandment, that you love one another. Just as I have loved you, you also should love one another" (John 13:34).

Don't you find it interesting that when Jesus spoke about obeying the commandments, he almost always spoke in terms of love? "If you love me," he said, "you will keep my commandments" — not primarily out of obligation, you see, not out of guilt, not out of fear, but out of love. "If you *love* me, you will keep my commandments." That's the challenge he puts before us, a demanding challenge to be sure.

But the challenge is made easier because of the promise that accompanies it. "I will not leave you orphaned" (John 14:18), he says. I will not leave you alone. No, you are part of my family, and "I will ask the Father and he will give you another Advocate to be with you forever" (John 14:16).

Some time ago I heard a young man speak at the funeral for his grandfather. The young man told the congregation that he was adopted but had always sensed that his grandfather loved him as much as the other grandkids, none of whom was adopted. To illustrate his point, the young man told of the time that he, his grandfather, and his father all went to a major league sporting event. At halftime they bumped into a man who had been the grandfather's business associate years before. The man, not knowing that the grandson was adopted, looked at the three generations — grandfather, father, and son — and said, "Wow! I can sure see the family resemblance. All of you look so much alike." With that, the grandfather put his arm on his grandson's shoulder and said simply, "Yes, we all do look alike, don't we?" At that moment, recalled the young man during the funeral eulogy, I knew beyond the shadow of a doubt that my grandfather loved me unconditionally and that I was part of the family.

As disciples, we are part of the family of Jesus Christ. He has adopted us into his family. He has given us the promise of his presence to guide us and sustain us when we venture out into the world, which, as we've seen, is a terrible and a dangerous place. He challenges us to live lives that give glory to the family name, the name of Christ, not by defining ourselves according to the world's standards, but according to the standards of Christ. He challenges us to stand apart from the world and to try to transform it. "If you love me," he says, "you will show that love by keeping my commandments."

---

1. Joseph Sittler, *Gravity And Grace*, ed. Linda-Marie Delloff (Minneapolis: Augsburg Publishing House, 1986), p. 6.

2. Edna St. Vincent Millay, "God's World" in *Contemporary Poetry*, ed. H. Lincoln Foster (New York: The Macmillan Company Publishers, 1963), p. 28.

3. This is a phrase which Eugene Peterson uses in his paraphrase of the New Testament called *The Message* (Colorado Springs: NavPress, 1993), p. 151.

4. Quoted in R. Maurice Boyd, *A Lover's Quarrel With The World* (Philadelphia: The Westminster Press, 1985), p. 13.

**Ascension Of The Lord
Luke 24:44-53**

The Three Ws
Of The Christian Life

Following the resurrection of their Lord, the disciples' lives must have been an emotional roller coaster. On the one hand, they had the Easter assurance that Christ was not dead but alive. "Why do you look for the living among the dead?" asked the Easter angels. "He has *risen*" (Luke 24:5). On the other hand, however, the Good News of the resurrection also meant that the earthly Jesus whom the disciples had come to know and love would no longer be with them. "Why do you look for the living among the dead?" said those angels. "He is *not here*, but has risen." In other words, the Good News of the resurrection may have felt like bad news to those who wanted to hold on to that familiar, fleshy Christ.

Better than any of the other Gospels, the Gospel of Luke explores this double-edged dilemma in its concluding verses. Jesus has been raised — hallelujah! Jesus is no longer with us — what in the world do we do now?

What in the world do we do now? How are we supposed to live our lives now that Jesus has gone to sit at the right hand of God? Today's reading from the Gospel of Luke explores this dilemma, and part of what it suggests is this — *wait*. "Stay in the city," says Christ to his disciples. "Stay in the city until you have been clothed with power from on high" (Luke 24:49). Admittedly, this command to wait seems strange and startling to people like us who live in a fast food, "I want it now" culture. Do you like to wait? I don't. For example, when I go to the doctor's office for a 3:30 appointment, I want to see the doctor at 3:30. But no, the receptionist says, "The doctor had an emergency and is running late. Why don't you just sit down and wait?" No wonder they call the reception area in the doctor's office the *waiting* room!

People who study such things tell us that we Americans spend five years of our lives waiting in lines: the line to buy textbooks for your college classes, the line to register your car or apply for a marriage license, the line to order a fast-food lunch, the line to get tickets for the symphony, even the line to greet the preacher after church! On top of that we spend nearly six months of our lives waiting for the traffic light to turn green.[1] Most of us spend far too much time waiting as it is. And now we are told that waiting is also part of the life of faith?

But it is! The prophets of Israel looked out into the future and said, "Things may be bad now. But when the Messiah comes it will all be different ... so wait." Hundreds of years later the Holy Spirit came upon the Virgin Mary, says the Gospel story. The power of the Most High God overshadowed her. And then she had to wait — nine long months — to give birth to the Hope of the world. Did that newborn child begin right away to act like the Messiah? Probably not! Undoubtedly, there was more waiting to do until the child grew through his early years, through adolescence, and through the so-called "silent years." Finally, when he was in his early thirties, he stood in the River Jordan and was baptized by John as a voice from heaven proclaimed him the dearly loved Son.

He preached about something called the kingdom or the reign of God, but we're still waiting for that kingdom to arrive in all of its fullness and, of course, we pray for it to come each time we say the Lord's Prayer. "Thy kingdom come ..." we pray. And as we pray, we wait. He broke bread with his disciples in a meal we have come to call the Last Supper, and he promised us that whenever we eat the bread and drink from the cup we proclaim our Lord's death until he comes again. For his return, we continue to wait. He promised the presence of the Holy Spirit to his followers and then instructed them to wait. "Stay in the city until you have been clothed with power from on high."

Of course, our waiting can take different forms; emotionally we can wait in a number of different ways. For example, here's a high school student who was just caught cheating on a final exam.

He's sitting in the school office waiting to explain himself to the principal. Can you see how his waiting is filled with fear and dread? Here's a young woman waiting by the phone. She and her husband have been trying to conceive a baby and finally they think they've succeeded. She's been to the doctor; they've run the tests. And now she's waiting for the results. Can you see how her waiting is filled with hope and expectation? Here's that young woman's mother. She too has been to the doctor, but her reason is not nearly so hopeful. She's discovered a lump and she's waiting for the test results. Her waiting is filled with anxiety.

Waiting for God is like waiting for news about that hoped-for pregnancy — hardly a time of dread and doom, but a time of expectation and excitement as you anticipate the new birth that God can bring about in you. "Stay in the city," says Christ to his disciples, wait there "until you have been clothed with power from on high."

Of course, Christ wanted that time of waiting to be more than passive waiting. It was meant to be a time of active waiting, a time of *witnessing*. "You are witnesses to these things," says Christ to his disciples (Luke 24:48). As you may know, the word "witness" has two different meanings. On the one hand, we witness something when we observe it, when we internalize it, when we experience it taking place. On the other hand, we also witness to what we have observed when we share our experience with another. As seminary professor Tom Long has written: "In the first case we become aware of some event; in the second case, we make others aware of that event." Professor Long goes on to say:

> *An unbreakable bond exists ... between these two meanings. One cannot witness in the second sense unless one has witnessed in the first sense. We give testimony only to that which we have experienced. We can bear witness only when we have been an eyewitness.*[2]

If this is true, then to be a witness to the Christian faith is not just a command to go out and tell others what we believe, it is first and foremost an invitation to learn, to study, to grow. Unless you have an experience of faith, you cannot testify to the faith. Unless you receive, you have nothing to share. Unless you take in, you have nothing to give out.

Perhaps you've heard the old parable about the Holy Land. There are two seas there. One of those seas is fresh and clean and filled with fish. Trees surround the banks of the sea, and their roots reach down into the rich moist soil to draw nourishment from the ground. Birds build their nests near the water's edge, families build their homes there, and the children play along the water's edge. The River Jordan flows into this sea with sparkling water from the hills around Palestine.

The River Jordan flows south to another sea as well. Here the fish don't splash, the birds don't sing, and families almost never make their homes by the water's edge. The water is bitter in this sea, so no one drinks from it, and the air above is so thick you can practically cut it with a knife.

What could the difference be between these two seas? It's not the River Jordan — it empties the same clean, clear water into both of them. Nor is the climate the difference — it's basically the same for both. The difference is this. The Sea of Galilee does not keep the water it receives from the River Jordan. For every drop that flows in, another drop flows out. The receiving and the giving go on in equal measure. But the other sea is different. It keeps every drop of water it receives, giving none of it up. The Sea of Galilee gives and lives. The other sea gives nothing. It is dead, and is named, appropriately, the Dead Sea.[3]

To be a witness to the Christian faith is much the same. The giving and the receiving, the taking in and the giving out, need to go on in equal measure. If you are always on the receiving end, then your life will grow stagnant and stale. And if you are always on the giving end, then your spiritual well will eventually run dry until you have nothing left to give. To be a witness to the Christian faith requires balance — the receiving and the giving need to occur in equal measure: education *and* mission; spiritual growth *and* service; Bible study *and* evangelism.

These, then, are two of the *W*s of the Christian life — waiting and witnessing. And the third of them is *worship*. "While Jesus was blessing them, he withdrew from them and was carried up into heaven. And they worshiped him and returned to Jerusalem with great joy and they were continually in the temple blessing God" (Luke 24:51-52).

Here are two observations about worship and the first of them is this: worship is one of the most natural things that we humans do. Go anywhere in the world — even to the most remote location — and you will find human beings participating in some form of worship or another. Douglas John Hall, the Canadian theologian, offers this observation: "... no tribe of *Homo sapiens* or its forerunners has ever been located that did not worship some deity." Indeed, says Hall, we might "name our species *Homo religiosus* (the religious species) just as accurately as *Homo sapiens*."[4] Not only that, but our human ability to worship is one of the things that distinguish us from all other life forms on planet earth. Think about it. No other living thing is capable of worship. Pets like dogs are capable of devotion, of loyalty, of affection, but not of worship. Our Golden Retriever comes close, of course, especially when it's time for dinner and she bows down to the one who feeds her, but even dogs, among the most loving of pets, are not capable of worship. Worship is one of the unique attributes of being human; it is one of the things that set us apart from every other living creature. To worship is one of the most natural things that we humans do.

But worship, at least at this time in American history, is also one of the most unusual things that we do. Some people speak about going to church today as the consummate counter cultural activity, the thing that sets us Christians apart from everybody else. Indeed, in an essay in *The Washington Post*, Henry Brinton, a Presbyterian pastor, says, "Sabbath keeping seems like a very subversive activity, because it coos 'play' when the world shouts 'work.' "[5] Recently, a friend of mine told me about a man all dressed up in a suit and tie who went outside one Sunday morning to get in his car. A neighbor, still in his bathrobe, was picking up the newspaper when he spotted the man in his suit. "Where are you going dressed up like that, to work?" asked the neighbor. How sad that this neighbor had not a clue that the man was actually on his way to worship.[6]

Here's a test for you to conduct. The next time you drive to church on Sunday morning, survey the neighborhood. Determine how many of your neighbors are going off to church. Undoubtedly, many of them are not. Instead, they are cutting the grass, working in the garden, drinking a second cup of coffee as they read the Sunday newspaper, going for a ride on the nearby bike trail, playing golf, going to the beach, and so on.

A married couple from my former congregation attended an overnight office party at a downtown hotel. On Saturday night some of the participants were planning to get together for brunch the next morning. But my friends said, "We'll have to take a rain check. We're going to head back home early so we can go to church." "You're going to go *where?*" asked the astonished others. How revealing that attending worship has fallen so far out of favor.

But maybe that's not all that bad, because these days most of us who attend worship come for the right reasons not because of guilt or fear of eternal damnation; not because it will help us to advance our career; and certainly not because attending worship is the socially acceptable thing to do, because, frankly, these days it's just as acceptable to go to Sunday brunch and then go shopping at the mall.

Rather, we come because we *want* to come. We come because we believe that worship enriches our life. We come to give thanks and praise to the One from whom all blessings flow. We come because we believe that worship puts us in touch with the power of God that sends us out into the world to witness to our faith in both word and deed.

Waiting, witnessing, and worshiping. Can't you see how they are all interrelated and how they all depend upon each other? Without them — all of them — the life of faith is incomplete.

---

1. Quoted from "Sometimes Life Is a Big Waste" from *The Chicago Tribune*, June 21, 1988.

2. Thomas G. Long, *The Witness Of Preaching* (Louisville: Westminster/John Knox Press, 1989), p. 78.

3. Portions of this parable can be found in Leslie Weatherhead, *Steady In An Unsteady World*, Stephen A. Odom, ed. (Valley Forge, Pennsylvania: Judson Press, 1986), p. 125.

4. Douglas John Hall, *Why Christian? For Those On The Edges Of Faith* (Minneapolis: Fortress Press, 1998), pp. 18-19.

5. Henry G. Brinton, "God Rested, And So Should We" in *The Washington Post*, August 9, 1999, section B2.

6. This story was shared by Gary W. Charles, pastor of the Old Presbyterian Meeting House in Alexandria, Virginia, who is writing a book about the ways contemporary Christians worship, serve, study, and belong.

Easter 7
John 17:1-11

Praying For The Church

"Dear friends," is the way she began her letter ...

> *Dear friends,*
> *I was waiting to use a pay phone, when a young man came up to me, handed me some change and a slip of paper and said, "Take this money and dial the phone number on this piece of paper — it will help you if you need help. If not, it will do you a lot of good to listen." I was about to refuse because I was afraid that the young man was not well when I noticed the tears in his eyes and the sincere tone of his voice. So I took the money and told him I would make the call. He said to me, "Thank you, Lady. I was about to do something foolish with my life but that number really saved me." With that, the young man walked away.*
> *My curiosity got the better of me, so I approached the phone, put in the money and dialed the number. I was just about to say, "Hello," when a voice answered and said, "This is one of the ministers from Westminster Church responding to your Dial-A-Prayer request. Let us pray ..." The tape recording of the minister's prayer was filled with comfort and assurance and I can see why it brought such peace of mind to that troubled young man.*

Many of us have experienced something like that — the feeling that comes over us when we know that somebody has been praying for us. Those facing surgery enter the operating room with greater confidence knowing that friends and family are praying for them. Those who survive cancer or some horrendous accident will often say, "I believe that all of those prayers said for me made a huge difference." Those who experience some dark night of the soul or walk through the valley of the shadow of death find great comfort when someone says, "I'll be praying for you." Even ministers — or perhaps we should say *especially* ministers — draw strength from the prayers of others. "Tell me what day you write your sermons," she said, "and I'll be sure to pray for you then." Is anything more wonderful than knowing that somebody is praying for you?

Maybe there is. What may be even more wonderful is when the One praying for you is none other than Jesus himself. The disciples experienced his prayers firsthand. He had gathered them in the Upper Room, you recall, where he began to prepare them for his departure. He picked up a towel and a basin of water and washed their feet. "I have set you an example," he said to them, "that you also should do as I have done to you" (John 13:15). He gave them a new commandment: "... love one another. Just as I have loved you, you also should love one another" (John 13:34). He told them about the many dwelling places in the Father's house and how he was going to prepare a place for them. He warned them to be wary of the world and its corrupting influences, and he challenged them to define themselves, not according to the standards of the world but according to the standards of the gospel. "If you love me," he said to them, "you will keep my commandments" (John 14:15). He gave them the promise of his presence, the presence of the Advocate — the Holy Spirit — to be with them forever. He warned them about the persecution they would face (John 16:2). And then he prayed for them.

The seventeenth chapter of the Gospel of John records that prayer, in which Jesus prays first for himself and his own impending "glorification" on the cross. Then he prays for his disciples. Finally, he prays for all of the future faithful — people like us, in fact — who one day would receive the gospel message like a fine family heirloom which has been passed on lovingly from one generation to the next. It is a wonderful prayer, but even more wonderful is the knowledge that he prayed it for his disciples and for us and, therefore, for the church. There is nothing more wonderful than knowing that somebody is praying for you, especially when that somebody is Jesus.

According to the seventeenth chapter of John, Jesus prays for a number of specific things: for safety and protection, for the joy of faith, for victory over the powers of darkness. But the one thing he prays for twice is for *unity*, for oneness. For the disciples he prays, "Protect them, so that they may be one, as we are one" (John 17:11). Later, when praying for the future faithful, he asks, "... that they may all be one" (John 17:21).

If there is one prayer which we Christians have always needed it is the prayer for unity. Clearly, the disciples needed a prayer for unity. Sometimes we think that the disciples were one big happy family, but such an assumption is far from the truth. Just remember whom Jesus invited to be his closest friends and followers. For example, one of them was Levi who is sometimes called Matthew the tax collector. No one was more hated in Jesus' day than a Jew who had gone to work for the Romans, collecting taxes from his own people to turn over to Caesar. Can you picture Matthew walking to work in the morning, the neighbors looking the other way as he passes by, the children spitting in his path or throwing stones at him, the neighborhood dogs growling at him in anger — even their dog food is taxed! There was no one in Jewish society more despised than a Jew who had sold out to collect taxes for the Romans, and Matthew was one of them.

Sitting there in that Upper Room was another of Jesus' disciples, Simon the Zealot. We don't know much about Simon; the New Testament just doesn't say. But we do know something about the Zealots. The Zealots were intensely committed religious nationalists, a kind of John Birch Society of the ancient world. Completely dedicated to Jewish law and custom, they hated foreigners, especially the Romans who were taxing the lifeblood out of the Jews the way the British taxed the colonists before the Boston Tea

Party. Undoubtedly, Simon hated tax collectors like Matthew nearly as much as he hated Romans.

Yet here they are in the Upper Room, Matthew the tax collector with his briefcase stuffed with 1040 forms and Schedule Cs, and Simon the Zealot with his lapel button which says, "Palestine — Love It or Leave It"! Can there be any doubt why Jesus felt the need to pray for the unity of the disciples? Unity would be a struggle, even among his closest followers.

Some 2,000 years have come and gone and we modern-day disciples of Jesus are still struggling for unity. We continue to fall short of the high hope of our Lord's Upper Room prayer for oneness. Not long ago a minister described his recent trip to the Church of the Holy Sepulchre in Jerusalem, which was built on the very place where tradition says Jesus was crucified and then raised from the dead. That church should be a place of intense spiritual vitality and power and for many people it is. But what other people experience there is not the power of the gospel which overcame the grave but contentious clusters of Christians each claiming this sacred site as their own. It is like a war-zone "where this group claims this part of the church and that group claims that part." Said the minister:

> *The church is such a battleground that for the last hundred years or so, they haven't even let Christians have keys to the place. Instead, a certain Muslim family has been charged with keeping the keys, and when things get really bad, they just lock it up!*[1]

And what can we say about the Catholics and Protestants in Northern Ireland who are forever fighting with each other? What can we say about the history of Protestantism with its constant quarreling between denominations and even within denominations with one church breaking away from others, sometimes over large issues and sometimes over small issues? What do all of these denomination disputes say about the unity of the Church other than that somehow we have fallen short of the unity for which Christ prayed in the Upper Room? Will we ever resolve our deep divisions over issues like abortion and homosexuality and the methods we use to interpret the Bible?

"The glory that you have given me," Jesus prayed to God, "I have given them, so that they may be one, as we are one ... so that the world may know that you have sent me" (John 17:22-23). This is why Jesus prayed for unity — not so that diverse Christians can sip coffee out of paper cups at the fellowship hour after church, nor so that we might all be the same — unity does not mean uniformity. Rather, Christ prayed for Christian unity so that the world might know that God sent Christ. Our Christian unity is supposed to say something to the world about our evangelical witness to the uniqueness of Jesus Christ.

The Good News which John spells out in the seventeenth chapter of his Gospel is that the Risen Christ continues to pray for us, continues to foresee our unity when all we can see is division and dispute. In this regard, he reminds me of a certain minister whose custom it was to visit all the patients in the local nursing home whether they were members of his congregation or not. One of those patients was a young man in his thirties who was confined to the nursing home because of an injury to his brain. He lived his life in a coma-like state, unable to respond to anybody or anything. One day the parents of the young man came to visit and found this minister — this stranger — sitting in a chair by their son's bed. The minister was talking to their son — *as if* the son could understand. Then he read scripture to the son — *as if* the son could hear it. Then he prayed for the son — *as if* the son could know that he was praying. The father wanted to say to the minister, "You fool, don't you know about our son?" But then it dawned on him that the minister did know. He knew all along. He cared for their son *as if* the son were whole, because he saw him through the eyes of faith and, therefore, saw him as already healed.[2]

Christ sees the church the way that minister saw the young man, not as the fractured and fragmented fellowship that we so often are, but as the unified body of believers that we by God's grace are yet to become. And so he continues to pray for us, that some day we will all be one, and not so much one in doctrine, but one in Spirit, one in respect for one another, one in love for one another and for the world. As the old spiritual puts it, "They'll know we are Christians" — not by our uniformity of doctrine. Rather, "They'll know we are Christians by our love, by our love. Yes, they'll know we are Christian by our love." And miracle of miracles, Christ's prayers for our unity are making a profound difference.

On World Communion Sunday in 1998, 2,000 people jammed into Rockefeller Chapel at the University of Chicago as leaders from four major Protestant denominations gathered to celebrate what they hold in common. On that historic occasion the Evangelical Lutheran Church in America, the Presbyterian Church (U.S.A.), the Reformed Church in America, and the United Church of Christ took one step closer together in the long quest for Christian unity. One of the leaders confessed:

> *Part of the meaning of this day has to do with the historic blindness of our traditions to one another ... God opened [our] eyes to see that the disagreements that divided were in fact differences that need not divide.*[3]

The following year, on Reformation Sunday 1999, the anniversary of the day when Martin Luther nailed his Ninety-five Theses to the church door in Wittenberg, Germany, effectively launching what came to be known as the Protestant Reformation, Lutherans and Roman Catholics signed an historic agreement. The agreement attempts to reconcile differences of belief concerning "justification by grace through faith," a doctrine which has been one of the major points of contention between Catholics and Protestants for the last 482 years. A professor of theology from Catholic University in Washington, D.C., observed:

> *This document appears to be saying that the doctrine that Luther thought was central to the Reformation, and which led him to undertake it, is not one on which there are serious enough differences between Catholics and Lutherans to justify the division of the church.*[4]

The risen Christ continues to pray for the unity of Christians, and little by little those prayers are bearing fruit. There is nothing more wonderful than knowing that someone is praying for you, unless that Someone is none other than Christ himself!

1. Theodore J. Wardlaw of Central Presbyterian Church, Atlanta, offered this description in a sermon he preached at the General Assembly of the Presbyterian Church (U.S.A.), June 25, 1999.

2. This story in told by Thomas G. Long in *Preaching Biblically*, Don M. Wardlaw, ed. (Philadelphia: The Westminster Press, 1983), p. 99.

3. Quoted in *The Christian Century*, October 21, 1998, p. 959.

4. See Charles Trueheart, "Faiths Heal Ancient Rift Over Faith" in *The Washington Post*, November 1, 1999, p. A1.

Books In This Cycle A Series

GOSPEL SET

It's News To Me! Messages Of Hope For Those Who Haven't Heard
Sermons For Advent/Christmas/Epiphany
Linda Schiphorst McCoy

Tears Of Sadness, Tears Of Gladness
Sermons For Lent/Easter
Albert G. Butzer, III

Pentecost Fire: Preaching Community In Seasons Of Change
Sermons For Sundays After Pentecost (First Third)
Schuyler Rhodes

Questions Of Faith
Sermons For Sundays After Pentecost (Middle Third)
Marilyn Saure Breckenridge

The Home Stretch: Matthew's Vision Of Servanthood In The End-Time
Sermons For Sundays After Pentecost (Last Third)
Mary Sue Dehmlow Dreier

FIRST LESSON SET

Long Time Coming!
Sermons For Advent/Christmas/Epiphany
Stephen M. Crotts

Restoring The Future
Sermons For Lent/Easter
Robert J. Elder

Formed By A Dream
Sermons For Sundays After Pentecost (First Third)
Kristin Borsgard Wee

Living On One Day's Rations
Sermons For Sundays After Pentecost (Middle Third)
Douglas B. Bailey

Let's Get Committed
Sermons For Sundays After Pentecost (Last Third)
Derl G. Keefer

SECOND LESSON SET
Holy E-Mail
Sermons For Advent/Christmas/Epiphany
Dallas A. Brauninger

Access To High Hope
Sermons For Lent/Easter
Harry N. Huxhold

Acting On The Absurd
Sermons For Sundays After Pentecost (First Third)
Gary L. Carver

A Call To Love
Sermons For Sundays After Pentecost (Middle Third)
Tom M. Garrison

Distinctively Different
Sermons For Sundays After Pentecost (Last Third)
Gary L. Carver

www.ingramcontent.com/pod-product-compliance
Lightning Source LLC
LaVergne TN
LVHW051655080426
835511LV00017B/2589